WHO GOT GAME?

P9-CFT-108

BASEBALL

AMAZING BUT TRUE STORIES!

BY **Derrick Barnes**

ILLUSTRATED BY **John John Bajet**

Cherry Tree Elementary
Media Center
Carmel, IN 46033

WORKMAN PUBLISHING ★ NEW YORK

TO THE

KANSAS CITY URBAN YOUTH ACADEMY—

*CONTINUE SPREADING THE MAGIC OF BASEBALL
AND SOFTBALL THROUGHOUT THE MIDWEST.
ROYALSURBANYOUTHACADEMY.COM*

—DB

TO MY

MOM, DAD, AND OLDER BROTHERS—

*THANK YOU FOR THE LOVE AND SUPPORT,
AND FOR ALL THE ART SUPPLIES.*

—JJB

- -

COPYRIGHT © 2020 BY DERRICK BARNES
ILLUSTRATION COPYRIGHT © 2020 BY JOHN JOHN BAJET

ALL RIGHTS RESERVED. NO PORTION OF THIS BOOK MAY BE REPRODUCED—
MECHANICALLY, ELECTRONICALLY, OR BY ANY OTHER MEANS, INCLUDING
PHOTOCOPYING—WITHOUT WRITTEN PERMISSION OF THE PUBLISHER. PUBLISHED
SIMULTANEOUSLY IN CANADA BY THOMAS ALLEN & SON LIMITED.

LIBRARY OF CONGRESS CATALOGING-IN-PUBLICATION DATA IS AVAILABLE.
ISBN 978-1-5235-0553-1

DESIGN BY SARA CORBETT
ADDITIONAL CREDIT: BAMLOU/DIGITALVISION VECTORS/GETTY IMAGES P. 42 (MAP)

WORKMAN BOOKS ARE AVAILABLE AT SPECIAL DISCOUNTS WHEN PURCHASED
IN BULK FOR PREMIUMS AND SALES PROMOTIONS AS WELL AS FOR FUND-RAISING
OR EDUCATIONAL USE. SPECIAL EDITIONS OR BOOK EXCERPTS CAN ALSO BE CREATED
TO SPECIFICATION. FOR DETAILS, CONTACT THE SPECIAL SALES DIRECTOR AT
THE ADDRESS BELOW OR SEND AN EMAIL TO SPECIALMARKETS@WORKMAN.COM.

WORKMAN PUBLISHING CO., INC.
225 VARICK STREET
NEW YORK, NY 10014-4381
WORKMAN.COM

WORKMAN IS A REGISTERED TRADEMARK OF WORKMAN PUBLISHING CO., INC.

PRINTED IN CHINA
FIRST PRINTING FEBRUARY 2020

10 9 8 7 6 5 4 3 2 1

Contents

CHAPTER 4

Colossal Comebacks

Who Got Game?

Well, it might be someone that you didn't even know existed. Until now. This book is about the unrecognized and unheralded figures and the untold stories that hold important spaces in baseball history. Here are forty-two priceless tidbits, astronomical stats, untouchable records, unforgettable plays, hilarious stories, and some of the most important baseball folks you've probably never heard of.

Like the teen girl who struck out two Baseball Hall of Fame greats in an exhibition game. Or the real home-run king who lived not in the US, but in Japan. Or the longest game ever played in baseball history.

Once you've read this and consumed it, PLEASE share these valuable, shiny nuggets far and wide. In the meantime . . .

PLAY BALL!

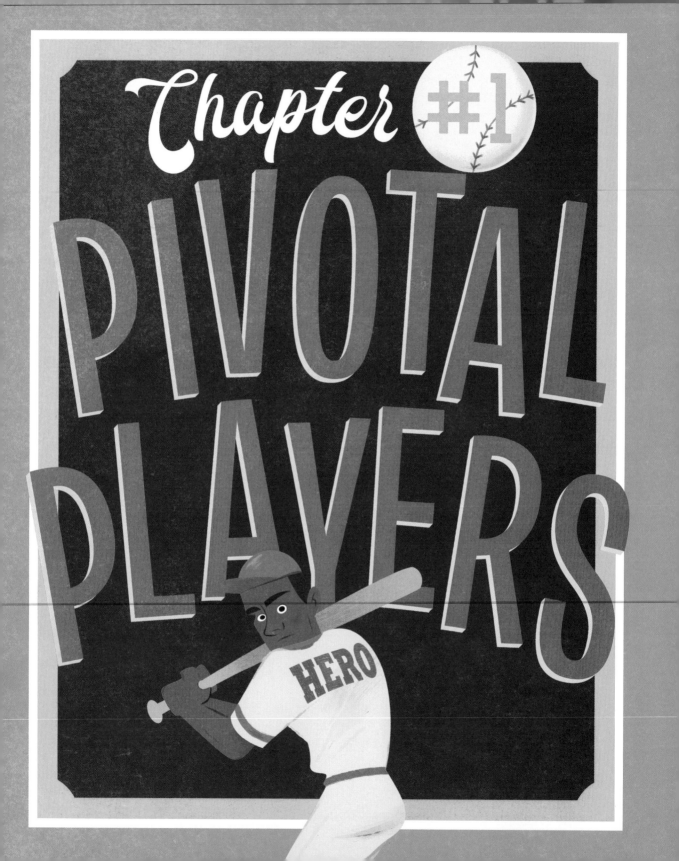

Let's put some shine on a group of very important people in baseball who almost never get the recognition they deserve. Some are mold-makers, the prototypes, the first of their kind. Others are mold-*breakers*, the ones who did the seemingly impossible. People who saw the way things always were and thought, *there's a better way.*

These are the innovators, both on and off the field. The inventors of new playing styles, new scoring techniques, new ways to overcome devastating injuries. They are so pivotal to the game, that today you can still hear echoes of the things they did back then.

Don't worry if you don't know their names— you will! Learn them, remember their stories, then tell everyone you meet!

There was a time when official team baseball was considered a game for White men only. But that didn't stop women and people of color from picking up a bat and taking a swing. In fact, in the 1860s, around the time of the Civil War, a number of all-Black baseball teams popped up throughout the country. Teams like the Philadelphia Pythians, the Bachelor Base Ball Club of Albany, and the Brooklyn Unique played against each other in an unofficial way. Over the next twenty years, there were more than 200 Black ball clubs all over the country, traveling from town to town to play one another. But there was no organized league, no way to tell who was the best of the best—or at least the best in a region. An incredible visionary—and pretty amazing pitcher—named **ANDREW "RUBE" FOSTER** wanted to change that. Thanks to his undeniable talent and unrelenting drive, he is now known as the father of the Negro Leagues.

The legend of Rube Foster, the pride of Calvert, Texas, began in 1897 when he joined an all-Black team called the Waco Yellow Jackets at the age of seventeen. Tall and powerful, he quickly became known for his blazing fastball and his wicked screwball.

A screwball, one of the most difficult pitches to throw, is the opposite of a curveball. A curveball, if thrown with the right hand, arcs out to the right then swoops back down and in toward home plate. But a screwball, even if thrown with the right hand, arcs inside, and then swoops down into the catcher's mitt. Crazy, right?

When major league teams came to Texas for spring training, Rube would practice with the White players. He impressed the teams with his talent. They impressed him with how organized and professional they were.

At the time, Black teams were a little all over the place. Some had unusually short seasons. Others folded because of financial issues. And players were always jumping from one team to the next. Rube himself played for three different teams during the 1902 season: the Giants in Chicago, a semi-pro White team in Michigan called the Independents, and the Cuban X-Giants. None of this team-hopping slowed Rube down—he ended the season with a 44–0 winning streak.

For the next three years, Rube threw fire. But being on the

field wasn't enough for Rube—he wanted a piece of the behind-the-scenes action, too. He went back to Chicago, and in 1907 became player-manager of his old team, now called the Leland Giants. Three years later, he left the Leland Giants and started his own team, the Chicago American Giants, made up of players from the Leland Giants and the Philadelphia Giants (giants were apparently very popular back then). Over the next few years, he grew his team into a powerhouse, even securing a home field—a ballpark once owned by the Chicago White Sox.

In 1920, at a Kansas City YMCA, Rube arranged a meeting with seven owners of other all-Black teams from the Midwest. Together they formed the first Black baseball league: the Negro National League (NNL), with Rube as president and treasurer. The league consisted of eight teams: the American Giants (Chicago), Chicago Giants, Dayton Marcos, Detroit Stars, Indianapolis ABCs, Kansas City Monarchs, St. Louis Giants, and Cuban Stars. Some NNL teams drew larger crowds than the White major league teams, inspiring Black teams in other parts of the country to form their own leagues. Rube worked hard to maintain the NNL until he became ill in the late 1920s.

The league continued after his death in 1930, but was never quite the same.

Between 1920 and 1960, six other Negro Leagues were formed. Then, in 1947, Jackie Robinson left the Kansas City Monarchs (an all-Black team that was first part of the NNL, and later part of the Negro American League) to become the first Black player in the Major Leagues. Robinson paved the way for twenty Black players to move from the Negro Leagues to the Major Leagues in the next four years, and the need for the Negro Leagues diminished.

The "Negro League" was not one unified group of teams. It was seven loosely connected leagues that existed from 1920 to 1960. They included:

- ★ **THE NEGRO NATIONAL LEAGUE I** *(1920–1931)*
- ★ **THE NEGRO NATIONAL LEAGUE II** *(1933–1948)*
- ★ **THE EASTERN COLORED LEAGUE** *(1923–1928)*
- ★ **THE AMERICAN NEGRO LEAGUE** *(1929)*
- ★ **THE EAST-WEST LEAGUE** *(1932)*
- ★ **THE NEGRO SOUTHERN LEAGUE** *(1932)*
- ★ **THE NEGRO AMERICAN LEAGUE** *(1937–1960)**

The first championship was played in 1924 between the Kansas City Monarchs of the NNL and the Hilldale Club of the Eastern Colored League. The Kansas City Monarchs won, five games to four.

*1960 IS THE ACCEPTED END DATE, BUT THERE'S SOME DISPUTE AS TO WHETHER IT ENDED EARLIER.

Currently, thirty-five players from the Negro Leagues have been inducted into the Baseball Hall of Fame, including Rube Foster.

During an immigration wave that began in the 1880s, the Jewish population in the United States grew by about two million people. Some Americans worried about competing with Jewish immigrants for jobs, housing, and other resources. Across the United States, communities passed laws limiting the rights of Jewish people. Some laws prevented them from buying houses in certain neighborhoods. Others banned them from country clubs and hotels.

Then, in the 1930s, Adolf Hitler came to power in Germany and inflicted horrific violence upon German Jews. Many fled for their lives, and over 300,000 Jews sought refuge in the United States. But by 1938, after decades of trying to discourage immigration, the United States government would allow only 27,370 German immigrants a year to enter the country.

Against this backdrop of anti-Semitism (discrimination against Jewish people), Detroit's Hammerin' Hank Greenberg, the first Jewish American player inducted into the Baseball Hall of Fame, became a legend.

Hammerin' Hank was a bona fide power hitter. In his 13-season career, he racked up 331 homers and 1,274 RBIs.

He led the American League in home runs four times in his career (1935, 1938, 1940, and 1946), and he won the Most Valuable Player award twice (in 1935 and 1940). His skills with a bat made him one of the most popular players of the time. Despite this, there were still people, fans and players alike, who taunted him and called him anti-Semitic names during games. But he just ignored them and sent the ball screaming out of the park.

Hank wasn't very religious, but he still appreciated the importance of tradition. In 1934, he became the first major leaguer to skip a game because of Yom Kippur, the holiest day of the Jewish year. And it wasn't just any game—his team, Detroit, was playing against the mighty Yankees during a pennant race (in other words—a chance to go to the World Series)! When Hank arrived at the synagogue for the Yom Kippur service, the entire congregation stood and gave him a round of applause.

Hank was also one of the first major leaguers to enlist in the Army to fight against Germany and its allies in World War II. At the time, he was the highest-paid player in the league, with a $55,000 annual salary. That would be close to a million dollars today, which isn't as much as the gigantic $200 to $300 million dollar–deals modern baseball stars get (see page 114), but back then that was a lot of money for a professional athlete. Yet, in 1942, Hank chose to give all that up to serve his country, missing nearly four full seasons.

When Hank returned to play with Detroit on July 1, 1945, it was as if he'd never left. In his first season-and-a half back, he tallied 57 homers and 187 RBIs! When Hank's fourteen-year baseball career came to an end, he was making close to $100,000 and was a five-time All-Star and a two-time World Series champion (1935, 1945). In 1956, he was inducted into the Hall of Fame.

In 1947, Hank was one of the first players to publicly welcome Jackie Robinson to the majors.

OZZIE VIRGIL

THE FIRST DOMINICAN PLAYER IN THE MAJORS

Out of the 882 Major League Baseball (MLB) players who took the field on opening day in 2019, a whopping 251 were born outside of the United States. The country with the greatest representation—102 players—was the Dominican Republic. Who was the maverick, the trailblazer, the first to come from the small Caribbean nation on the island of Hispaniola (the Dominican Republic is on the east side, Haiti is on the west) and open the door for so many others? New York Giant **OZZIE VIRGIL**.

Virgil's family emigrated to the United States in 1945 when he was only thirteen. They settled in the Bronx in New York, where Virgil went to DeWitt Clinton High School. Because he didn't make his school's baseball team, he had to settle for playing sandlot ball (which is another way of saying he played with his friends). Once he graduated, Virgil signed up for the US Marine Corps Reserves and played for their team at Camp Lejeune, North Carolina. He focused on being an all-around talent and learned as many positions as he could. (The only two he didn't learn were center field and pitcher.) Virgil served in the Reserves for two years, and when he got home, he was good enough to try out for the New York Giants.

Virgil made his debut with the Giants on September 23, 1956, becoming the first Dominican to play major league baseball. He played for six teams over nine seasons, mostly as a "utility man." That means he was a backup for multiple positions and played wherever and whenever he was needed. His numbers were not flashy (174 hits, .231 batting average, 73 RBIs, and 14 home runs all in 324 games), but they were good enough to prove that he could hang with the big boys, and he helped open the doors for other Dominican and Latinx players. Felipe Alou, the second Dominican to play in the majors, joined the

FELIPE ALOU

Giants in 1958 and became an All-Star player. Juan Marichal joined the same squad in 1960 and became a Hall of Fame pitcher.

From the late 1960s to the early 1970s, there was a significant increase in Latinx players on teams like the Braves, Pirates, Reds, White Sox, and Indians. Many Dominican players compare Virgil's importance to that of Jackie Robinson's for Black players. But Virgil, charming and humble, would say, "I have always felt grateful and fortunate to have been chosen by God to open the doors of baseball for my countrymen, considering that hundreds with more talent than me hadn't been given the chance."

JUAN MARICHAL

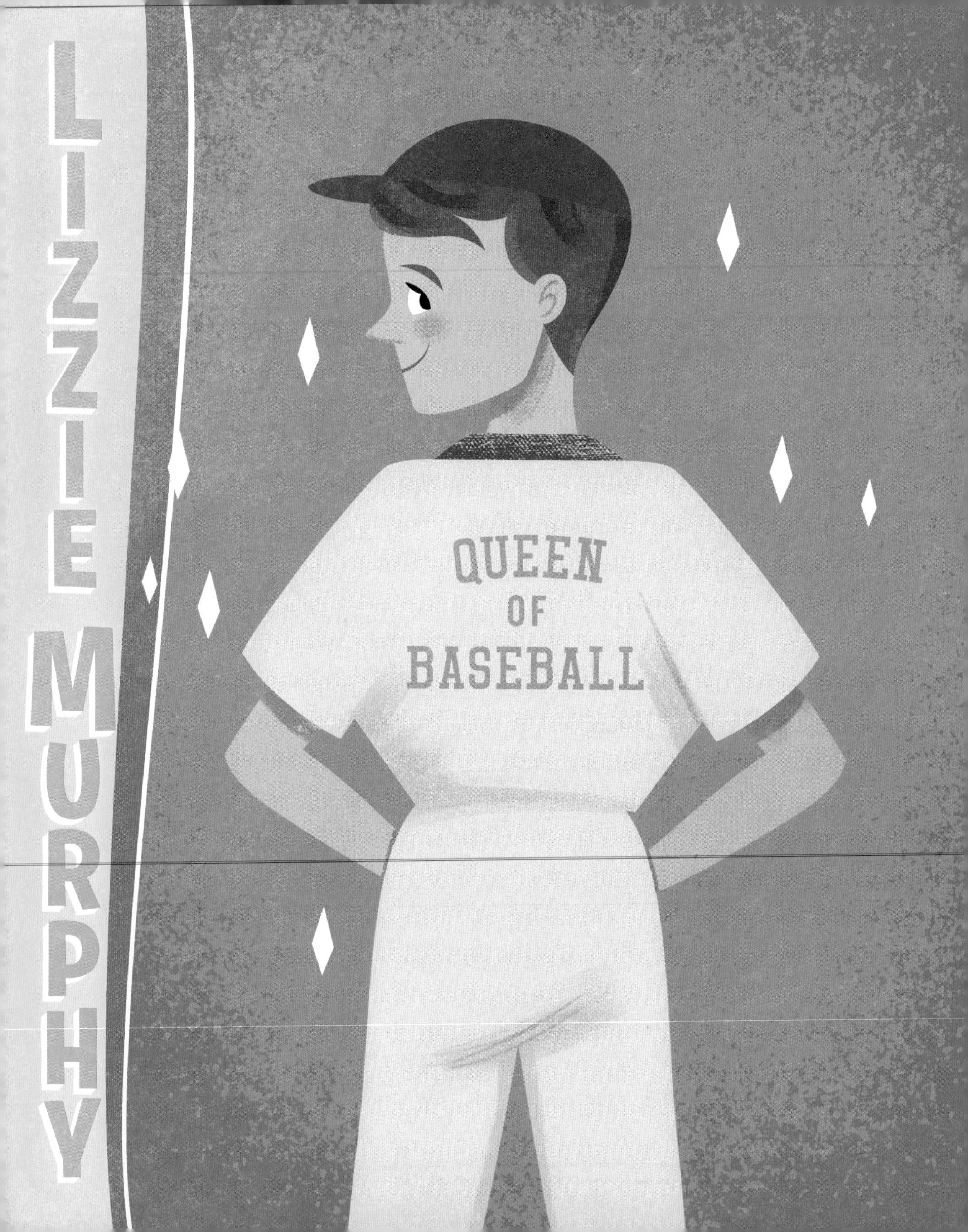
LIZZIE MURPHY
QUEEN OF BASEBALL

The history of women playing baseball goes all the way back to at least the 1860s, when Vassar College in Poughkeepsie, New York, hosted the first all-women teams. Then in the 1890s, the Bloomer Girls appeared—teams of women who traveled from town to town playing hardball. In 1943, as more and more major league players went to fight in World War II, the All-American Girls Professional Baseball League was founded. It was the first pro sports league exclusively for women. Throughout this rich history of women in baseball, there was one pioneer who really set herself apart. Self-promoting superstar **LIZZIE MURPHY** was the first woman to play on a major league team.

Murphy, who also called herself "Spike," grew up in Rhode Island in the early 1900s. She played every single sport she could—hockey, track, swimming, skating—more than holding her own with the boys. But don't get it twisted—Lizzie wasn't just an athlete. She was also fluent in French, loved to cook, and played the violin. But athletics were where she really shone.

By the time Lizzie was fifteen, she was playing on a few amateur baseball teams, and at eighteen, she played professionally for the Providence Independents. But in 1918, she stepped out of her comfort zone, left the friendly confines of Rhode Island, and signed with a coed traveling squad called Ed Carr's All-Stars of Boston. They played at least one hundred games a year in New England and Canada, and Lizzie was the clear-cut star. Fans loved to watch her dominate on the diamond, but she was determined to dominate off the diamond as well.

At the time, most amateur baseball players didn't make enough money playing ball to support themselves and had jobs on the side. But the star players made enough money to live on, and Lizzie knew she was a star. Early in her career she negotiated a fee of $5 per game and a percentage of the money collected from ticket sales. Between innings, she also sold postcards announcing herself as "the Queen of Baseball." And to make sure people didn't forget her name (as if they could) Lizzie had it stitched across the front AND back of her jersey. Brilliant. (Teams didn't start putting names on the backs of jerseys until 1960, when baseball became a popular sport to watch on television. Lizzie was ahead of her time!)

Lizzie would do anything to grow her star (and financial) power. In 1922, she played first base for Ed Carr's All-Stars of Boston in a charity game against the American League's mighty Boston Red Sox. Six years later, she played on a National League All-Star team in another major league exhibition game, this time against the Boston Braves of the National League. This appearance made her the first woman to play on a major league team.

Despite all her efforts, baseball never did bring Lizzie the financial security she hoped for. In the nearly twenty years she was with the All-Stars of Boston, Lizzie maintained a .300 batting average. She retired at the age of forty and went to work on oyster boats. What a colorful life.

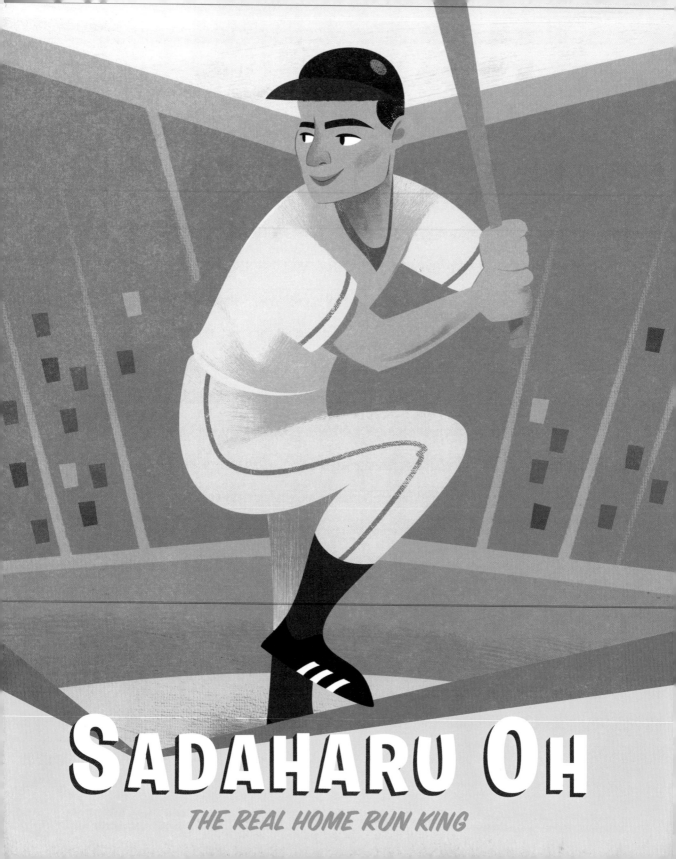

SADAHARU OH

THE REAL HOME RUN KING

When people mention the Mount Rushmore of Power Hitters, they often think of the same names: Hank Aaron (755 homers), Barry Bonds (762), Babe Ruth (714), and Alex Rodriguez (696). But there was someone with a mightier swing than all of those guys. This guy has 113 more homers than the legendary Hank Aaron! Who was this mad batter? **SADAHARU OH**, the master of the big swing.

Sadaharu Oh began his baseball career right out of high school, signing with Japan's Yomiuri Giants. At fourteen he pitched a no-hit, no-run game in the national play-offs, so he was bummed when the Giants told him his smaller size made him better suited for hitting. But he went with the flow, became a first baseman, and gave up pitching.

After a rocky start, Oh worked hard to perfect his power swing. He practiced the martial art of Aikido, which emphasizes harmony, motion, and movement. From Aikido, Oh learned to take his time with his swing and to control his hips.

He also practiced Zen, a daily habit of peace, meditation, and self-control. Zen helped Oh create a unique hitting stance called the "flamingo." While he waited for a pitch, Oh stood on one leg.

When he swung at the ball he planted his foot at the same time, which gave him balance, leverage, and power.

His opponents thought his stance was weird, but the fans loved it. Plus, it was effective. In his rookie season, Oh hit only 7 home runs. But after his training, he averaged 43 homers per year. In fourteen of his twenty-two seasons, he hit over 100 RBIs a season. At the end of his career, he tallied 2,170 RBIs, 2,786 hits, and a .301 batting average to go with his record 868 home runs.

Oh's critics say that the ballparks are smaller in Japan and

In the early 1870s, after the Civil War, a Union soldier named Horace Wilson (he fought the Confederacy in Louisiana—so hooray for him!), traveled to Japan to teach English. While he was there, Horace taught his students a little game called baseball. Word got out, and soon baseball was popular throughout the country, especially as other American teachers in Japan taught it to their students.

In the years following World War II, the sport became even more popular. Many of the American soldiers who stayed in Japan after the war ended helped spread the joy and wonderment that is baseball.

that Oh was up against less talented pitchers than those in the majors. But hey, I bet if he had had the opportunity to play baseball in the United States, his face would be right up there on the Mount Rushmore of home run hitters.

Oh later became a successful manager with the Yomiuri Giants between 1984 and 1988. He was inducted into the Japanese Baseball Hall of Fame in 1994. He even won, as a manager of an All-Star national team, the inaugural World Baseball Classic in 2006 against Cuba.

HANK AARON

BABE RUTH

BARRY BONDS

SADAHARU OH

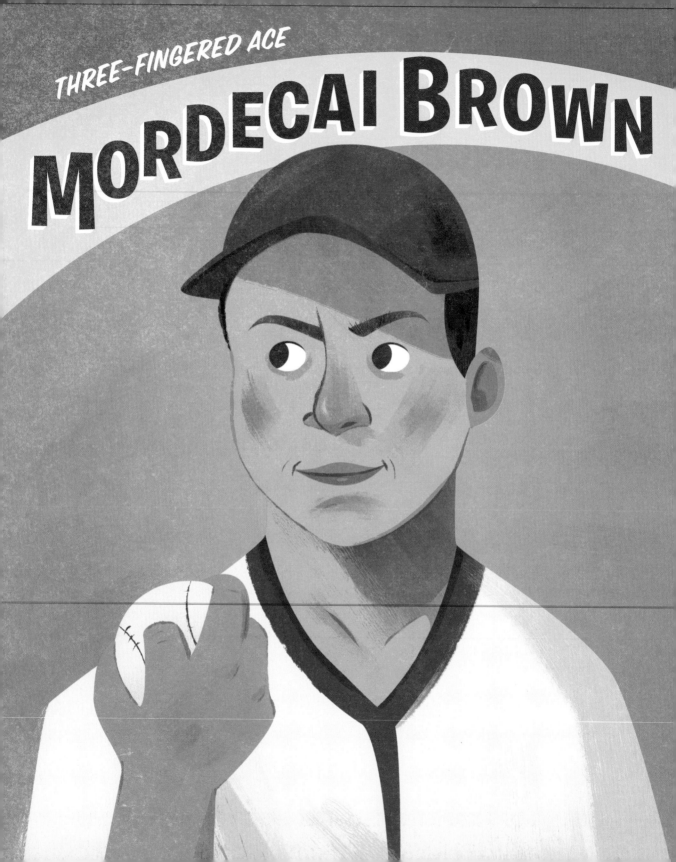

THREE-FINGERED ACE

MORDECAI BROWN

Baseball has a long tradition of welcoming players with physical disabilities onto the field. As a matter of fact, Topps, the largest baseball trading card company, released a special collection of baseball cards in 2015 called "Pride & Perseverance." The cards featured current and former ballplayers who overcame physical challenges to do great things. Players like pitcher Jim Abbott, who played from 1989 to 1999 and pitched a no-hitter in 1993 despite being born without a right hand. Pete Gray, the "One-Armed Wonder," played for the St. Louis Browns in 1945, and outfielder Curtis Pride, a former thirteen-year MLB player, who was born deaf. But the first major league star with a disability was Hall of Fame pitcher **MORDECAI PETER CENTENNIAL BROWN**.

Born in Nyesville, Indiana, Mordecai suffered two life-altering accidents as a kid. First, his right index finger was sliced off in a machine made for separating corn and grain. The next year, he fell while chasing a rabbit and broke the remaining fingers on his right hand, leaving him with a bent middle finger and a paralyzed little finger. But this didn't keep him from developing a passion for baseball.

Mordecai was a coal miner and played baseball just for fun. He worked hard to perfect a grip with his thumb and three fingers and developed a way of holding the ball that gave his pitches more movement and greater rotation. In other words, his pitches were extremely challenging for batters to hit. Mordecai dominated the small amateur league in Terre Haute, Indiana, and finally gained enough attention to make his major league debut with the St. Louis Cardinals on April 19, 1903, against the Chicago Cubs.

The next season, Mordecai was traded to the Chicago Cubs. By that time he had developed a wicked, deceptive, downward curveball that few batters could hit. Hall of Famer Ty Cobb once said Mordecai's pitch "was the most deceiving, the most devastating pitch I ever faced." That signature pitch garnered Mordecai a 15–10 record and an awesome 1.86 earned run average (ERA) in his first season with the Cubs. Over the next seven years, he averaged almost twenty-four wins per season. He even helped the Cubs take home two world championships in 1907 and 1908.

Over his magnificent fourteen-year career, Mordecai played in nine World Series games, with a 5–4 record and a 2.97 ERA. He still holds the lowest career ERA—1.93—in the history of the National League. And in 1949, Mr. Brown was inducted into the Baseball Hall of Fame.

Before 1974, if you wore out your elbow from years and years of throwing pitches, you were pretty much done. The pain of this "dead-arm injury" caused lots of pitchers to retire before their prime. But in 1974, an orthopedic surgeon named **DR. FRANK JOBE** developed a treatment that changed the fortunes of baseball pitchers forever.

Growing up, Dr. Jobe wasn't all that athletic. But he had steady hands and long, thin fingers—perfect for a surgeon. After serving in the Army, Dr. Jobe went to medical school, where he studied under Dr. Robert Kerlan, the doc for the Los Angeles Dodgers. He kept working with Dr. Kerlan after he graduated, and eventually became the Dodgers' official orthopedic (muscle and bone) surgeon in 1968.

Around this time, Dr. Jobe saw the great Dodgers pitcher Sandy Koufax struggle with an elbow injury. Doctors didn't know what to do other than tell him to rest and ice his arm. But the pain proved too great, and Koufax had to retire in his prime.

Dr. Jobe thought that Koufax's trouble might have to do with the ligaments (stretchy bands that hold bones together) in his elbow. He'd read about doctors who replaced injured tendons (stretchy bands that connect muscle and bone) in one part of the body with healthy tendons from another part. Could this have helped Sandy Koufax?

The ligament that controls elbow movement is called the ulnar collateral ligament or UCL. It is made up of three bands that connect the upper arm bone (called the humerus) to the larger of two bones in the lower arm (also known as the ulna). If the UCL is torn or stretched (often resulting in great pain), the bones aren't held together tightly, and the arm is harder to control. Kind of a big deal if you're a pitcher!

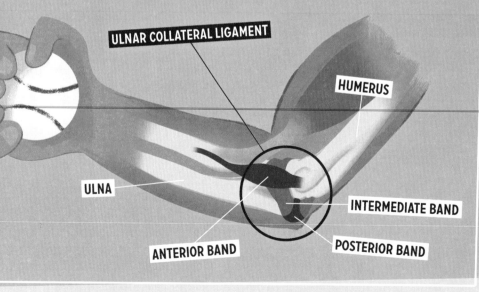

ULNAR COLLATERAL LIGAMENT

HUMERUS

ULNA

INTERMEDIATE BAND

ANTERIOR BAND

POSTERIOR BAND

One night in 1974, Dr. Jobe watched as star Dodgers pitcher Tommy John took the mound. John was a lefty with a 13–3 record and a 2.59 ERA in 22 starts. But that night, Tommy threw two out-of-control pitches back-to-back. Later, Tommy said he heard a *POP!* as he threw the second pitch, and felt like his arm wasn't there. He had torn a ligament in his left elbow, an injury that might have ended his career. Enter Dr. Jobe!

He replaced the torn ligament in Tommy's left arm with a tendon from his right forearm. Yeah, Doc was very experimental. It took Tommy nineteen months to recover from his ulnar collateral ligament reconstruction (try saying that six times fast!), but he returned to play in the 1976 season. The surgery was such a success that Tommy went on to win 164 more games over the following fourteen seasons. He retired from the game at the age of forty-six.

No procedure has saved more pitchers' careers than Tommy John surgery, as it came to be known. Dr. Jobe was inducted into the Hall of Fame in 2013.

Many historians and fans consider **LEROY ROBERT "SATCHEL" PAIGE**, a Mobile, Alabama, native, the greatest pitcher who ever lived. He was a Negro League god who became a major league rookie at the tender age of forty-two! He was way past his prime, but still able to stand on any baseball mound and toss heat to batters half his age.

The legend of Satchel Paige was real. He was a tall, right-handed pitcher with long limbs and a smooth delivery. He could toss every single pitch in the book with ease. He was also a real showman. Sometimes he would stare down a batter, wind up, then pause right in the middle of the pitch. Baffled batters would swing and miss. Every single time. The "Hesitation Pitch," as it was called, was very popular with fans, but eventually the pitch was outlawed.

Satch made up other pitches too, with names like the "Bat Dodger," "Thoughtful Stuff," "Long Tom," the "Bee-Ball," the "Midnight Creeper," the "Wobbly Ball," and the "Whipsy-Dipsy-Do." Sometimes, just for show, he'd call his outfielders in when a batter stepped to the plate, letting everyone know he didn't think the batter would hit what he was throwing. Then, just as predicted, he would strike the batter out.

During the 1942 Negro League World Series against the vaunted Homestead Grays, Satch famously claimed he walked two batters just so he could get a shot at power slugger Josh Gibson (in fact, records show that the batters got hits). Talk about confidence! Satch struck Big Josh out—1, 2, 3—of course.

Satch landed his first major league start six years later, in 1948, with the Cleveland Indians. That year, he helped the Indians make it to the World Series and became the first Black player to pitch in a major league championship. He went on to play for the St. Louis Browns. In 1965, at the age of fifty-nine, Satch pitched his last pro game with the Kansas City Athletics.

In his long career, Satch was a five-time Negro League All-Star and a two-time MLB All-Star. He was one of the first players from the Negro Leagues to win a world championship, and he was the first player from the Negro Leagues to be inducted into the Baseball Hall of Fame. If only Black players had had the chance to play in the major leagues before 1947! Satch might have rewritten the record books. Those who had a chance to see him play, or to play against him, hold the same opinion—he was the G.O.A.T. (greatest of all time).

Back in the early days of baseball, before the National League was created, there weren't many ways to keep track of the games, and almost no one was breaking down specific stats for hitting, pitching, or fielding. If not for the efforts of a writer named **HENRY CHADWICK**, baseball might have stayed a fun game between friends instead of becoming America's favorite pastime. Chadwick is considered the first serious journalist to cover the sport in depth, and his contributions made a serious impact on the way we understand the game today.

British-born Chadwick came to Brooklyn with his family in 1837 when he was twelve years old. Back home, he had been a big fan of the game of cricket, a bat-and-ball game that may have inspired baseball. At the age of twenty, Chadwick worked for a local newspaper, writing about cricket for British fans who loved the game and played it in the States. While covering a game at the Elysian Fields in Hoboken, New Jersey, Chadwick saw a few guys playing what would eventually become baseball. It was the most beautiful game Chadwick had ever seen.

Over the next few years, Chadwick wrote about this new game in great detail, coining phrases like *base hit, strikeout,* and *cutoff.* (A cutoff throw happens when the ball is too deep in the outfield for one person to throw it all the way to a base when trying to get someone out.) Chadwick was also the first to use the letter "K" to stand for a strike (because "K" is the last consonant in the word *strike*). Today, you can go to any baseball game and see fans holding up big signs with the letter "K" to intimidate batters and keep count of the strikeouts.

In 1859, Chadwick devised what might be his greatest contribution to baseball—the box score. The box score is a summary of a baseball game written in a chart. Today it includes a list of players and an abbreviated account of runs, hits, and errors. Numbers, stats, records, and dates play such a big role in baseball, more so, arguably, than in any other sport. It's the oldest organized sport in America, and the stats go a long way in helping to build the legends and keep track of records that sometimes last for decades. In other words, the box score and other statistical documentation keep track of baseball history.

Chadwick was inducted into the Baseball Hall of Fame by a special committee in 1938.

EAGLES
OF RED HOOK

Names	O	R
Smith	3	2
Peragine	4	1
Leary	0	4
Bobbins	3	1
Katz	1	2
Torres	4	0
Kwon	4	1
Archibald	5	0
Griffith	3	1
	27	12

HOUNDS
OF NEWPORT

Names	O	R
Bobowicz	3	1
Elliott	2	0
Santos	3	1
Lyon	1	2
Edwards	2	0
Todd	4	1
Beakings	3	0
Smolevich	5	2
Duffy	2	0
	27	7

Home runs—Hounds, 3; Eagles, 4.
Fly catches—Hounds, 11; Eagles, 12.
Umpire—D. Cooper, Kittendale, New York.
Scorers—Logge and Kiley.
Time—Three hours and twenty-four minutes.

METS 1, PHILLIES 0

PHILADELPHIA	AB	R	H	RBI	BB	SO	AVG
Rollins SS	4	0	0	0	0	0	.243
Polanco 3B-2B	4	0	0	0	0	2	.317
Ibanez LF	3	0	0	0	0	1	.271
Sweeney, M 1B	3	0	0	0	0	1	.265
Werth RF	3	0	0	0	0	1	.301
Victorino CF	3	0	0	0	0	1	.248
Schneider C	3	0	0	0	0	0	.226
Valdez, W 2B	1	0	0	0	1	1	.253
A Dobbs PH-3B	1	0	0	0	0	0	.190
Hamels P	2	0	0	0	0	0	.160
B Brown, D PH	1	0	1	0	0	0	.225
TOTALS	28	0	1	0	1	7	.260

NY METS	AB	R	H	RBI	BB	SO	AVG
Reyes, Jo SS	4	0	0	0	0	1	.222
Pagan LF	4	0	1	0	0	0	.306
Wright, D 3B	4	1	1	0	0	0	.287
Beltran CF	4	0	1	1	0	2	.216
Hessman 1B	4	0	1	0	1	1	.167
Francoeur RF	4	0	0	0	0	1	.237
Blanco, H C	4	0	1	0	0	1	.267
Tejada 2B	4	0	0	0	1	2	.183
Dickey P	4	0	0	0	0	0	.172
TOTALS	29	1	5	1	2	8	.249

Back in Henry Chadwick's day, box scores only recorded outs (O) and runs (R). These days, box scores offer a lot more information. From the number of at bats (AB) to the number of RBIs to how many times a player walked (BB) or struck out (SO), today's box scores are snapshots of the entire game.

KIM NG

THE HIGHEST-RANKING WOMAN
IN BASEBALL . . . SO FAR

Since the beginning of the game, women have been fighting for their place in baseball—not just on the field, but off the field as well. There is a whole network of powerful people who make big decisions behind the scenes—which players are hired for your favorite team, for example. For most of baseball history, powerful positions were held exclusively by men. Finally, in 1990, Elaine Weddington Steward was hired as the assistant general manager (GM) for the Boston Red Sox, becoming the first woman to hold an executive position in Major League Baseball. Eight years later, **KIM NG** was named assistant general manger for the Yankees. Ng was a bold and brilliant assistant general manager, but she didn't stop there. Now a senior executive with Major League Baseball, Ng is both the highest-ranking woman and the highest-ranking Asian American in the sport.

Ng was an MVP softball infielder at the University of Chicago, but she never imagined a career in professional sports. (She thought she'd be an investment banker like her mom.) On a whim she applied for (and got) an internship with the Chicago White Sox in 1990. Within a year, she flipped that internship into a full-time job with the club. The Sox's general manager at the time, Dan Evans, was impressed with Ng. Her fresh ideas and her strong work ethic convinced Evans that Ng had a long and successful career ahead of her.

Over the next four years, Ng worked her way up the ladder, becoming Assistant Director of Baseball Operations for the Sox. In this role, she dealt with players—scouting new talent, negotiating contracts, and helping decide who should be traded. In 1995, at the age of twenty-six, Ng became the first woman, and the youngest person ever, to negotiate on behalf of a major league club in a salary dispute with a player. From there, her career shot into the stratosphere.

When the New York Yankees hired Ng as assistant general manager in 1998, she became responsible for negotiating big-time contracts with All-Star players like Derek Jeter. Instead of just looking at a player's stats to determine his worth (as was typically done), Ng considered personality and leadership skills—strengths you wouldn't see if you just looked at numbers on a chart. Ng's approach to re-signing top talent, like players Mariano Rivera and Paul O'Neill, helped the Yankees win three World Series.

Ng left the Yankees to work with her old boss Dan Evans as vice president and assistant general manager of the LA Dodgers. She oversaw the Dodgers' whole minor league system. In 2011, she left the Dodgers to become Senior Vice President of Baseball Operations for all of Major League Baseball. In this role, Ng oversees all international baseball operations, such as player development and scouting in Asia and in countries like Mexico, Venezuela, and the Dominican Republic.

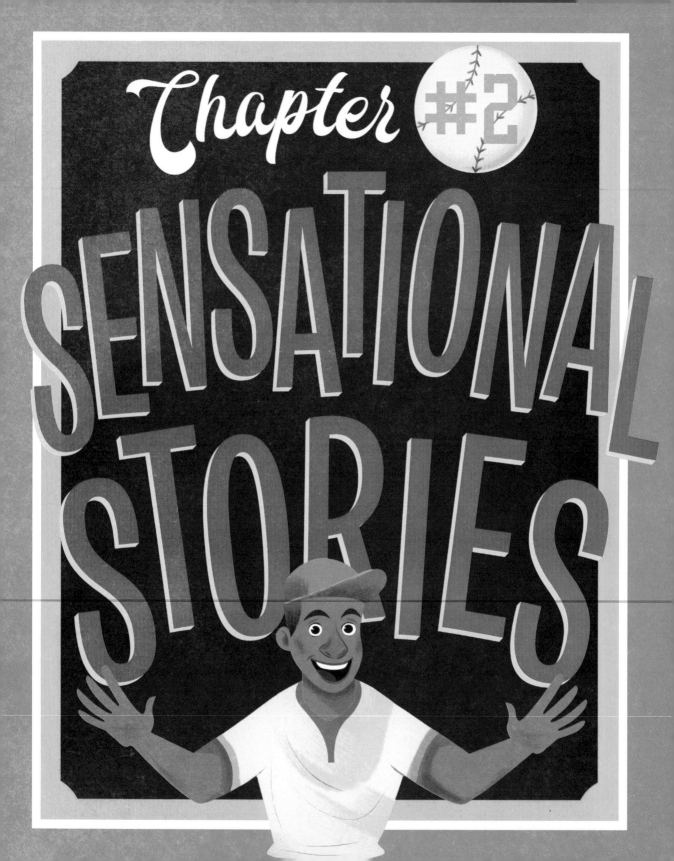

**Y**ou've met the pillars of the sport—the absolute greats. Learned all about their amazing accomplishments and ground-breaking ideas. Now get ready for the juicy stuff—the good, bad, honorable, and well, embarrassing stories that make baseball the big, sloppy, magnificent mess that it is. Moments that made wide-eyed, slack-jawed fans turn to each other and say, "Did you see that?!" Stories grandfolks tell their grandkids again and again because *they were there.*

You'll meet players who took real risks for their place on the field. And true heroes who put love of country above their love of the game.

So here's to the moments that make baseball great! They're not all pretty, but they certainly are memorable.

THE SPITBALL

The **SPITBALL** was pretty much what it sounded like—a ball covered in grossness. All that slime helped the ball slide off the pitcher's fingers more quickly and easily. Over the course of a game, the ball would get dirtier and dirtier, making it harder for batters to see. If a batter didn't get out of the way in time, he'd get hit, sometimes hard enough to take him out of the game. Thanks to one really dirty spitball, Cleveland Indians shortstop Ray Chapman was taken out of the game for good.

Ray Chapman was a fan favorite. He was fast and great on the field. Before he showed up in 1912, the Indians had never finished in first place in the American League. But in 1920 they did, thanks in part to the 97 runs Chapman scored.

On August 16, the Indians played the first of a three-game series against the Yanks. It was the top of the fifth when Chapman stepped up to the plate that foggy August afternoon. He crouched down in his signature stance and waited for Yankee pitcher Carl Mays to throw the ball. Mays was known for slathering his pitches with slobber, and he threw a spitball that hit Chapman on the left side of his head. It hit hard enough for the fans to hear and traveled far enough after hitting Chapman's head that Mays thought the ball was in play. He threw it to first before he realized what had really happened.

Chapman fell to the ground. His teammates carried him off the field. He had a severe skull fracture, and despite emergency surgery, Chapman passed away in the early hours of the next morning.

Even with this tragedy, it wasn't until 1934 that the spitball was outlawed for good. It was another twenty-two years after that before the National League would require all of their players to wear protective helmets. The American League followed suit two years later.

Ray Chapman is the only baseball player in the history of the game to die from an injury sustained during major league play.

MAJOR LEAGUE PLAYERS WHO ENLISTED IN WWII

World War II lasted six brutal years, from 1939 to 1945, and involved over thirty countries. The massive global conflict was sparked by Nazi Germany's 1939 invasion of Poland. Big-time allies Great Britain, France, and the Soviet Union (Russia) battled the "Axis" of Germany, Italy, and Japan. On December 7, 1941, the Imperial Japanese Navy Air Service launched a surprise attack on a US Naval base in Pearl Harbor, Hawaii. Now America had no choice but to enter the war, joining Great Britain and her allies. But the US needed soldiers. More than five hundred major league players and over four thousand minor league players heeded the call.

Many were drafted, meaning the government required them to serve. But others joined the armed forces voluntarily. So what happened to the sport when players decided to take up arms?

On January 14, 1942, the commissioner of baseball sent a letter to President Franklin D. Roosevelt asking whether or not he should shut down the games. The president responded the next day with what is now called the Green Light Letter. In the letter, Roosevelt said the games should continue because they would boost the spirits of the entire country during such a turbulent time. Which was true. There is nothing that eases the mind more than watching your favorite team take the field for a nine-inning slugfest with a rival, right?

So baseball chugged along. Major league teams filled their rosters with teenagers, veteran players (some long retired), and any reasonably fit guy who could catch, run, or hit. Even with the shortage, the majors refused to allow women or Black men to play ball, but in 1943 a separate league was founded just for women.

The major leagues also stole players from the minor leagues, causing their numbers to dwindle. There were thirty-one minor league teams in 1942, the year after the attack on Pearl Harbor. By 1943, there were only nine left. Major league farm systems (teams of young players not yet ready for the majors) were also vanishing; the St. Louis Cardinals' mighty minor league network shriveled to a mere six teams, while the Chicago White Sox didn't even have a minor league team in 1943.

When the war ended in 1945, many players returned to their respective teams. Unfortunately, a lot of them had been severely wounded in the war and could no longer play the game they loved so much.

Baseball players who put their careers and lives on hold to fight in World War II are prime examples of men who put duty and service to their country above all else. Here are a few of the legends who traded in their cleats and mitts for the uniforms of the armed forces. Salute!

★ **HANK GREENBERG, DETROIT TIGERS**
20th Bomber Command, US Army Air Force

★ **STAN MUSIAL, ST. LOUIS CARDINALS**
Seaman Second Class, US Navy

★ **JOE DIMAGGIO, NEW YORK YANKEES**
Staff Sergeant, US Army Air Force

★ **JACKIE ROBINSON, BROOKLYN DODGERS**
Second Lieutenant, 761st Tank Battalion, US Army, drafted before MLB career began

★ **ENOS SLAUGHTER, ST. LOUIS CARDINALS**
Sergeant, US Army Air Force

★ **MONTE IRVIN, NEGRO LEAGUE NEWARK EAGLES**
Sergeant, GS Engineers 1313th Battalion, US Army

★ **JERRY COLEMAN, NEW YORK YANKEES**
Pilot, US Marine Corps, postponed start with team to fight

★ **YOGI BERRA, NEW YORK YANKEES**
Seaman Second Class, US Navy

★ **TED WILLIAMS, BOSTON RED SOX**
Second Lieutenant, US Marine Corps

THE
Unfortunate Luck
OF
HUGHIE JENNINGS

By all accounts, Baltimore Orioles legend **HUGHIE JENNINGS** was a good man. He was a serviceable shortstop and first baseman and a pretty good manager and coach from 1891 to 1925. But ol' Hughie had a fiery, spirited personality that sometimes led to some pretty interesting moments, both on and off the field.

Hughie was a decent hitter with a .312 batting average, but he had a tendency to crowd home plate, meaning he'd lean into the strike zone, and was at greater risk of being hit. So much so that he still holds the record for being hit by the most pitches

during a season: 51 in 1896! In his whole career, he was hit by 287 pitches. OUCH! That's a painful record!

During a game in 1897, Hughie was struck in the temple by a fastball. His skull was fractured, and he was rushed to a local hospital where he lay unconscious for four days. Once he recovered, he was back on the field and continued to play baseball for several more years. His days as a full-time player ended with the Phillies in 1902. In 1903, he played six games with the Brooklyn Superbas (the modern-day LA Dodgers).

Even with his bad luck on the field, it was an incident OFF the field that made Hughie the most infamous. After his playing days were done, Hughie decided to pursue a legal degree at Cornell University. One cold winter evening in 1904, after a long day of studying, Hughie felt like a dip in Cornell's indoor pool and dove right in without checking to see if the water was fine—or even there! DUDE JUMPED HEAD FIRST INTO AN EMPTY POOL! He ended up with a serious head injury, two severely sprained wrists, and cuts and bruises all over his body. But he survived and became a very respected trial lawyer.

Practicing law was cool, but Hughie just couldn't stay away from the game he loved. He returned to baseball in 1907 and managed the Detroit Tigers for fourteen highly successful years. He left the Tigers with 1,131 wins under their belt, making him the winningest manager in the team's history (a record that stood until 1992).

Hughie was so admired for his ability to bounce back and overcome adversity that he earned a spot in the Baseball Hall of Fame in 1945. And Cornell University went on to invest in covers for every single pool on its campus. Just kidding. But they probably should have, right?

THE

"JUMBO WAGNER"

THE MOST EXPENSIVE TRADING CARD IN THE UNIVERSE

Legendary Pittsburgh Pirates shortstop **HONUS "THE FLYING DUTCHMAN" WAGNER** was one of the most dominant players of his era or any thereafter. Between 1897 and 1917, he was a World Series champion, won eight batting titles, led the league in slugging percentage six times (the slugging percentage is the total bases divided by the number of times the player was at bat), and stolen bases five times. Dude was a big deal. He was actually one of the first five players inducted into the Baseball Hall of Fame. So, it only made sense that when baseball trading cards became popular in the United States,

Honus Wagner's face would be printed on thousands. But that's not how it happened.

Cheap black and white baseball cards were produced by tobacco companies as early as the 1880s. Between 1909 and 1915, known as the "golden age of baseball cards," they started to resemble the colorful, stat-filled cards you see today.

One of the most valued and most popular series is the T206 or the "White Borders" series, created by the American Tobacco Company from 1909 to 1911. The full set contained 524 cards, most of which were of minor league players who never became big-time major league stars. But the set also included Hall of Fame players like Ty Cobb, Christy Mathewson, and, of course, Honus Wagner.

At that time, Wagner was the only player to object to the cards. He didn't like his image being sold with cigarettes, especially since kids looked up to him (good job, HW!). Plus, the American Tobacco Company either didn't pay the players for their likenesses, or paid very little.

The American Tobacco Company stopped production of the T206 Honus Wagner after printing somewhere between 50 and

200 cards (no one knows for sure), making them very rare. One was discovered in the 1970s by a collector in Vermont. It was called the "Jumbo Wagner" because it was larger than the other cards in the run. (Most T206 cards are 2⅝ inches in height. The Jumbo Wagner measures 1⁷⁄₁₆ inches by 2¹¹⁄₁₆ inches.) The Jumbo Wagner has been sold and resold over the years, and in 2016 it was auctioned off for a record $3.12 million.

So, run and tell your Uncle Randy to hold on to his card collection that he keeps in a hundred shoe boxes in your granny's basement. He just might have another T206. Who knows?

JACKIE MITCHELL

Legend-Slayer

Seventeen.

That's how old minor league pitcher **JACKIE MITCHELL** was when her team, the Chattanooga Lookouts, played an exhibition game against the mighty New York Yankees. That's how old she was when she struck out two of the mightiest Yankees of all time: Babe Ruth and Lou Gehrig.

Jackie was introduced to the game early on by her father, who took her out to the baseball field almost as soon as she learned how to walk. As she got older and learned to play, her next-door neighbor, Charles "Dazzy" Vance, an eventual Hall of Fame pitcher,

most notably for the Brooklyn Dodgers, became her coach. Dazzy led the National League in strikeouts seven seasons in a row (1922–1928), so you know Jackie was learning from one of the best.

At the age of seventeen, Jackie joined an all-girl team in Chattanooga, Tennessee, and attended a baseball training camp in Atlanta, Georgia. It was there that Joe Engel, owner of a minor league team called the Chattanooga Lookouts, saw what a talent she was. Joe was a big-time publicity guy who did everything he could to draw a crowd. And when he saw Jackie tossing some heat, he invited her to join his all-male team in a game that was the stuff of legend.

On April 2, 1931, in front of 4,000 fans, Babe Ruth walked to the plate, tipped his hat at Jackie, and smiled. His stance was relaxed, like he wasn't expecting much from a girl. Suddenly, Jackie hurled a wicked, left-arm pitch with a side delivery. Babe didn't swing, but his facial expression changed. It was a ball, but it showed that Jackie meant business! Jackie tossed another pitch, but this time Babe swung—and missed! He missed the next pitch too. Two strikes! The next pitch was sweet. Jackie delivered a sinker to the outside corner of the strike box, and Babe struck out. It only took 4 pitches to strike out one of the greatest power hitters of all time.

Next up was Lou Gehrig, the man known as "the Iron Horse." Gehrig was about to have a great season. He would tie Babe Ruth as the league leader in home runs that year and finish with a .341 batting average. Didn't matter. On that day, Gehrig swung and missed 3 straight pitches. The crowd went nuts.

Now, some historians say the whole thing was a prank, an (after) April Fool's Day gag. But neither Babe Ruth nor Lou Gehrig ever admitted to striking out on purpose. And Jackie Mitchell swore up and down until the day she died at the age of seventy-three that those two men swung with sincere force, and missed.

BEFORE JACKIE ROBINSON

Jackie Robinson will always get credit for being the first Black player who, in 1947, broke through the barrier that kept African Americans from playing major league baseball. But did you know that four Black players played professionally on all-White teams decades before J-Rob?! In other words, they were the first Black players to play minor or major league ball. Who were these four pioneers? **JOHN "BUD" FOWLER**, **WILLIAM EDWARD WHITE**, and brothers **MOSES FLEETWOOD WALKER** (what a cool name!) and **WELDY WILBERFORCE WALKER**.

In 1878, John "Bud" Fowler became the first Black player in organized baseball when he joined an all-White minor league team called the Lynn Live Oaks. Bud was a pretty well-rounded ballplayer—a superb pitcher, catcher, and considered by some to be the best second baseman in the land. But he bounced from team to team because at some point, someone—either one of his teammates, opponents, or the team's fans—would complain about a Black man playing on a White team. When this happened, Bud had to move on.

Bud liked playing organized baseball, and in the 1880s he tried to create a national Negro league. That didn't work out, and he spent the rest of his career playing for various White teams. His best seasons were in 1884 with a minor league team in Stillwater, Minnesota (he had a .302 batting average), and in 1890 when he played for a team in Galesberg, Illinois, and earned a .322 batting average.

Unlike Bud, William White played for one team—the Providence Grays—in one game, on June 21, 1879, against the Cleveland Blues. He had 4 at-bats, only hit the ball once, and scored 1 run. Nothing special, but he was there.

So who was William White? It's a bit of a mystery. His father was a White man, and his mother was an enslaved Black woman. According to the laws when he was born (1860), William was also considered Black and a slave. But here's the thing: When William died, his death certificate said he was a White man. William had light skin and straight hair, so it's possible people who saw him didn't know he was Black. And, because life as a White man was much, much easier than life as a Black man, it's possible William didn't correct them. Maybe that's how he got to play for the Providence Grays.

There was nothing mysterious about Moses Fleetwood Walker. On May 1, 1884, he hit the field for the Toledo Blue Stockings of the American Association. He had a decent year too (he batted .263 in forty-two games), considering all the racist treatment he endured. Walker almost made it through the entire season before bigoted fans, owners of other teams, and even a few White players began to complain. During an exhibition game in 1883, future Hall of Famer and Chicago White Stockings manager Cap Anson called Fleetwood a racial slur and refused to let his team play against the Blue Stockings. The nerve of that guy! When the manager of the Blue Stockings told Anson that his team had to play or go, Anson reluctantly agreed to let the White Stockings play. But from that point on, he led the effort to keep Black men out of Major League Baseball.

Two months later, Fleetwood's younger brother, Weldy Wilberforce Walker, was signed by the Toledo Blue Stockings. Toward the end of the season, the team received a letter threatening Fleetwood and Weldy's lives. They both decided to leave the team.

In July of 1887, Moses Fleetwood Walker and Cap Anson crossed paths again during an exhibition game between the Chicago White Stockings and Fleetwood's new club, the Newark Little Giants, a minor league team. Anson demanded that Fleetwood and another Black player be removed from the lineup. This time, the manager of the Little Giants agreed. That same day, all major league managers voted not to sign any more Black players. African Americans would not have the opportunity to play in the majors for another sixty years.

THE
PROBLEM WITH
STEVE BARTMAN

n October 14, 2003, the Chicago Cubs were one win away from the World Series—somewhere they had not been for a heart-wrenching fifty-eight years, and they hadn't won it in ninety-five years! They were at home, in the friendly confines of Wrigley Field, hosting the Florida Marlins in Game 6 of the National League Championship Series.

The Cubs had the lead, 3–0. It was the eighth inning, and the Marlins were at bat with one out. Marlins second baseman Luis Castillo hit a foul down the left field line. Cubs outfielder Moisés Alou jumped up to catch it, hoping to give the Cubs their second out. Instead, Cubs fan **STEVE BARTMAN** reached for the ball and missed, hitting the ball with his hand and preventing Alou from catching what would have been a definite out.

After that, the Cubs suffered a string of bad luck. They gave up 8 runs and ended up losing the stinking game 8–3. Isn't that something? And guess who the scapegoat was? You guessed it. Ol' Bart-boy. The TV camera stayed fixed on him as he seemed to shrink into his seat. Fans booed and poured drinks on him, and he had to be escorted from the stadium by security. Poor guy. He even had to have police cars outside of his house to keep the angry fans away. The next day, the Cubs lost Game 7, and *even though he wasn't there*, fans blamed Steve Bartman.

In 2016, the Cubs finally won that elusive championship, against the Cleveland Indians. To celebrate, Cubs chairman Thomas Ricketts had something special in mind for Steve Bartman. "On behalf of the entire Chicago Cubs organization," he said, "we are honored to present a 2016 World Series championship ring to Mr. Steve Bartman. We hope this provides closure on an unfortunate chapter of the story that has perpetuated throughout our quest to win a long-awaited World Series." Now that's real leadership.

ROBERTO CLEMENTE'S

LAST BIG REGULAR-SEASON HIT

nly thirty-two men in MLB history belong to the club of iconic ballers with 3,000 hits. They include Hank Aaron, Cal Ripken Jr., Pete Rose, Eddie Murray, Stan Musial, Lou Brock, and Ichiro Suzuki. Thirteen of these guys are left-handed, and two of them are switch-hitters. Six of them are also members of the very exclusive 500-home run club. But of all those ballers, only one player has *exactly* 3,000 hits: Pittsburgh Pirate **ROBERTO CLEMENTE**. His historic entry into the club is unique because it was his very last regular-season hit in a long, storied career.

On September 30, 1972, the world champion Pirates faced the New York Mets. It was one of the last games of the season before Pittsburgh headed to the playoffs. Roberto approached the plate in the bottom of the fourth inning. The crowd was on its feet. Mr. Clemente smacked the ball into left center field for a double— it was his 3,000th hit! The crowd erupted in applause! At the time, Clemente was only the eleventh person to reach such a milestone, and the first Latinx player ever. It was an amazing way to end the regular season.

Mr. Clemente was also well known for the philanthropic efforts he undertook in the off-season. On December 31, 1972, he was on a flight to help deliver food and aid to earthquake victims in Nicaragua when the plane's engine failed. The plane crashed into the Atlantic Ocean off the coast of Puerto Rico. Clemente's body was never found. He was thirty-eight years old.

On March 20, 1973, Roberto Enrique Clemente became the first Latinx player inducted into the Baseball Hall of Fame. His legacy lives on and serves as an inspiration for young Latinx ballplayers and as a reminder to all athletes to give more of themselves to those in need. The Roberto Clemente Award, voted on by fans and members of the media, is given out annually to a player who is an exceptionally helpful member of his community, exemplifies good sportsmanship, and is just a great teammate and ambassador for his squad. One player from each MLB team is nominated for the award. The winner is selected from that group of thirty guys and is announced during the World Series. Shout out to all of the athletes who, like Mr. Clemente, make their mark as solid human beings on and off the field.

33 SHORT INNINGS

THE LONGEST PROFESSIONAL GAME IN BASEBALL HISTORY

Today, the average baseball game is nine innings and lasts a little over three hours. Seems long, but nothing out of the ordinary. At least you get to stand up during the seventh-inning stretch, sing a song, shake your limbs, and keep your butt from becoming more numb than it already is. But can you imagine sitting for a game for over eight hours? Can you say numb buns?

On a cool, windy April evening in 1981, the minor league Triple-A Pawtucket Red Sox battled the Rochester Red Wings in front of a crowd of over 1,700 in Pawtucket, Rhode Island.

The game started half an hour late because of a few busted stadium lights. That was the first bad sign.

The game was scoreless until the top of the seventh inning, when Rochester scored on an RBI single. Then the boys from Pawtucket scored a last-minute run in the bottom of the ninth inning. The score was now 1–1. Neither team would score again until the twenty-first inning.

The tie was finally broken when Rochester scored at the top of the twenty-first. Pawtucket answered when Wade Boggs (who later became a Boston Red Sox legend and Hall of Famer) drove in a run in the bottom of the inning, tying the score again, 2–2. His teammates didn't know if they wanted to give him a high five or smack him in the face. At that point, everyone just wanted the game to end. It was so cold outside that the players burned wood from broken bats for heat.

The game went past midnight, into Easter morning. The players, managers, coaches, and the nineteen fans who remained were exhausted. Around 3:00 a.m., someone in the Pawtucket camp got fed up and called the league president, Harold Cooper. When they finally reached him, Cooper couldn't believe that the game was still going and ordered that it be stopped. It was 4:09 a.m., bottom of the thirty-second, and the score was tied at 2–2. The die-hard fans were given lifetime free passes to the stadium, which was pretty cool. President Cooper declared the game would continue on June 23. It only took one inning for Pawtucket to score, and the game finally came to an end with a final score of 3–2. It was a sellout game, with an enormous crowd of 5,746.

Obviously, the game made history by being the longest pro game ever, but during those eight hours and twenty-five minutes, thirteen other records were set: the most pitches (882), the most innings (33), the most at bats (by the Red Sox: 114), the most batters struck out (by the Red Wings: 34), the most plate appearances by one player in one game (including future MLB Hall of Famer and Orioles legend Cal Ripken Jr.: 15), and what was probably the most interesting record, the longest home plate appearance by one ump, Mr. Dennis Cregg, who continued as an ump for another twenty-eight years.

ROYALS LEGEND

GEORGE BRETT

AND THE
"PINE TAR INCIDENT"

PINE TAR has earned a place in Major League Baseball's sacred rule manual:

RULE 3.02(C): If pine tar extends past the 18-inch limitation, then the umpire, on his own initiative or if alerted by the opposing team, shall order the batter to use a different bat. The batter may use the bat later in the game only if the excess substance is removed.

Why the rule? Well, let's start by breaking down what pine tar is—a sticky, tacky, oozy substance used by batters to get a stronger grip on the bat. The better the grip, the better the swing.

The problem is, if the pine tar goes any higher than 18 inches on the bat, it can rub off on the ball when the batter hits it. The dirtier the ball gets, the harder it is to see. For the most part, the rule doesn't cause any hiccups, but there was a moment that did kick up some dust, and it involved one of the greatest hitters of all time, Kansas City Royals legend **GEORGE BRETT**.

On July 24, 1983, the Royals were playing in New York against the Yankees. The visitors were behind by a score of 4–3. There was one Royal on base, with two outs, in the top of the ninth inning. When George Brett headed to home plate to hit, he intended to send the ball soaring out of the park. And that's just what he did. He hit a two-run homer off the Yankees' ace relief pitcher, Goose Gossage, putting the Royals up 5–4. But the manager of the Yanks, Billy Martin, said, "Wait a minute,

Georgie boy!" He thought that Brett's bat had more pine tar on it than allowed, so he told the umpires.

After inspecting Brett's bat, the umpires decided that it was indeed in violation of the pine tar rule. They took back the homer and the two runs, which essentially gave the Yankees the win, seeing how it was the top of the ninth and the Yanks were ahead 4–3. When Brett heard the bad news, he charged at the umpires like a raging bull. He yelled, he hollered, he kicked up dust, and his eyes were stoked with fire. He was eventually ejected from the game, and the contest came to an end. The Yanks were victorious.

The Royals fought the call against Brett, and after some detective work, the American League ruled that the amount of pine tar was not excessive. The AL ordered that the game be replayed from the point when Brett was at bat. And on August 18 of that year, the Royals officially won. The final score was 5–4.

Chapter #3

RADICAL RECORDS

If the game of baseball is about nothing else, it's about numbers. More than any other sport, baseball is defined by the number of times a feat has been accomplished, repeated, and blown out of the water. Stats and records are really big deals.

Almost every baseball fan knows the biggies: home runs, strikeouts, RBIs (runs batted in), etc. But there are records and record holders that even the most hardcore baseball fan has never heard of. Do you know the number of father-and-son combinations or the number of relatives in the Hall of Fame? I bet your buddies don't know who the first MLB mascot was. Think your neighbor knows the story behind the highest scoring MLB game ever? Can the produce manager at your local grocery store tell you about the youngest player to ever appear in an MLB game? No? Well, get ready to school them all.

MR. MET

THE FIRST
MLB MASCOT

Some teams choose a mascot that fits their name, like Ace the Blue Jay of the Toronto Blue Jays. Others have mascots that have absolutely nothing to do with the team name, like the Arizona Diamondbacks. Their mascot is a bobcat instead of a snake. And then there are mascots that, quite frankly, look so weird and creepy that I wonder how they don't scare the daylights out of little kids. Have you seen the green, furry swamp thing called Southpaw from the Chicago White Sox? Three MLB clubs don't even have mascots: the Yankees and both teams from the Los Angeles area, the Angels and the

Dodgers. Apparently, they're too cool. But you know who's not too cool? The New York Mets. In fact, they were the very first MLB team to introduce a real-life mascot.

See, most baseball teams in the late 1800s had mascots, but they were not like the ones we know today. They were mostly cute little kids dressed in baseball uniforms, or animals, like a dog or a goat or something. The 1888 St. Louis Browns had both—a cute kid AND two dogs. Back then, mascots were considered good luck charms, not just comic relief or characters who throw free T-shirts into the crowd.

The New York Mets wanted to do something different with their mascot. A popular Marvel comic book creator named Al Avison contributed to the design, and a local costume company created a big, round baseball face that a person could just slide over their head. **MR. MET** debuted in April of 1964. (Some guy from the Mets ticket office named Dan Reilly volunteered to wear the costume.) It was the first time that an MLB team used a mascot in the stadium during a game. Soon, Mr. Met was plastered all over the Mets' yearbook, advertising material, the cover of game programs, and the Mets' scoreboard. Mr. Met was so popular that Mrs. Met was introduced in the late '60s.

But in 1979, the Mets decided they had had enough of Mr. Met and his bride. More children were coming to the games, and the Mets thought they needed a mascot that was more kid-friendly. Their solution? A mule. A stinking mule named Mettle. Mettle wasn't as popular as Mr. Met and lasted only one year.

The Mets remained without a mascot until 1992, when a lifelong, loyal Mets fan from Queens, New York, wrote the organization and begged them to give the big-headed embodiment of baseball joy another chance. Two years later, Mr. Met was back on the field. The fans rejoiced, and Mr. Met has been around ever since.

On September 14, 2007, Mr. Met was elected into the renowned Mascot Hall of Fame.

BABY NUXHALL

THE YOUNGEST PLAYER TO EVER START AN MLB GAME

I n 1944, while most of his buddies were hanging out at the soda shop and going to dances, a fifteen-year-old kid named **JOE NUXHALL** became the youngest person to ever play major league baseball.

Young Joe was a phenom in his hometown of Hamilton, Ohio. His dad was a ballplayer as well, but it was the younger Nuxhall who was known as a left-handed pitcher who tossed comets across home plate. Plus, at 6'2" and almost 200 pounds, he was hard to miss.

Nuxhall pitched for his high school and for his father's semi-pro team based in Hamilton. MLB scouts were itching to sign Nuxhall. Most major league rosters were depleted because of World War II (see page 50), and young Nuxhall was just what scouts were looking for. The general manager of the Cincinnati Reds scooped him up on February 18, 1944, after getting special permission from Joe's parents and high school principal.

Joe's first game was June 10, 1944. Unfortunately, the Reds were being hammered by the St. Louis Cardinals. By the bottom of the seventh inning, the Cards were up 11–0. By the ninth inning, Reds manager Bill McKechnie figured that since they were already down 13–0, why not put Joe in? What did they have to lose?

Joe was nervous. The first batter he faced grounded out. Then Joe gave up five walks, five runs, and two hits. The manager pulled him before the inning was over.

Joe was sent down to the minor leagues to work on his arm. But in 1945, he decided to go back home. Once he graduated from high school, he went back to the minor leagues, and in 1952, at the age of twenty-three, he rejoined the Reds.

By the end of his fifteen-year career, Nuxhall had an all-time record of 135–117, a 3.90 ERA, and was a two-time All-Star. He was inducted into the Cincinnati Reds Hall of Fame in 1968.

THE ONLY MLB PLAYER TO "HIT for the CYCLE" IN THE POSTSEASON

There are some things that only happen in baseball every once in a while. I'm talking about those rare accomplishments, like no-hitters; hitting four or more home runs in one game; stealing second, third, AND home in one game; or posting a .400 batting average for a season. When you think about how few players have actually accomplished these things versus the thousands who've played throughout MLB history, you can't help but tip your hat. Hitting for the cycle is that kind of feat.

Hitting for the cycle is when a batter hits a single, a double, a triple, and a home run in one game, in no particular order.

RADICAL RECORDS

The most times a player has hit for the cycle in their career is three times. Four guys have done it:

1 JOHN REILLY
Cincinnati Red Stockings and Cincinnati Reds first baseman
TWICE IN 1883, ONCE IN 1890

2 BOB MEUSEL
New York Yankees outfielder
ONCE IN 1921, 1922, 1928

3 BABE HERMAN
Brooklyn Robins and Chicago Cubs right fielder
TWICE IN 1931, ONCE IN 1933

4 ADRIÁN BELTRÉ
Seattle Mariners and Texas Rangers third baseman
ONCE IN 2008, 2012, 2015

HOME RUN
TRIPLE
DOUBLE
SINGLE

Another rare feat is pulling off a "natural" cycle. That's when a player has four hits in order: a single, double, triple, and then a homer. Only fourteen players have done it. You think that's something? Check *this* out. On May 25, 1882, utility player Curry Foley of the Buffalo Bisons hit for the cycle in order, but backward: He hit a homer in the first inning, popped a triple in the second inning, dinged a double in the fifth inning, and dinked a single in the seventh inning. Pretty cool, huh?

But do you know what's an even rarer cycle to hit, something that has only happened *once* in MLB history? Hitting for the cycle in the postseason. One. Time. Now that's really, really rare.

Red Sox utility player Brock Holt hit for his first cycle on June 16, 2015, in a regular-season game against the Atlanta Braves. When he did it the SECOND time, there was more on the line. It was Game 3 of the 2018 American League Division Series against the New York Yankees. Holt had already hit a single, double, and a triple. In the ninth inning, when it was his turn to bat, he hollered, "I need a homer!" as his teammates cheered him on.

The Red Sox were blowing the doors off the Yanks with a score of 14–1. At that point, New York basically gave up and wanted the game over with. They pulled all their pitchers and put in Austin Romine, a backup *catcher*, to finish the game. Romine got the first two outs of the inning, but then he walked Ian Kinsler. Holt came up, and Romine's very first pitch to him was a 79-mph sinker. Brock swung like a man possessed and sent the ball screaming deep into the right field grandstand. The Red Sox dugout went berserk! It was a two-run homer, and the first-ever postseason hit for the cycle! To top it all off, the Sox completely destroyed the Yanks 16–1.

The Boston squad went on to beat the LA Dodgers in the World Series and win their ninth world title.

The OG CREW

THE FIRST EIGHT TEAMS IN THE NATIONAL LEAGUE

When William A. Hulbert, owner and president of the Chicago White Stockings, founded the National League (NL) on February 2, 1876, there were eight clubs. It was not the first baseball league, but today it is the oldest professional sports league in the world. Clubs came and went, but by 1962, the National League as we know it began to take shape. That year, the Houston Colt .45s (later called the Astros) and the New York Mets joined the league. Seven years later, the Montreal Expos (now the Washington Nationals), and the San Diego Padres signed on. The Colorado Rockies and the Florida Marlins joined in 1993. Finally, the Arizona Diamondbacks and the Milwaukee Brewers (who switched from the American League—the first team to switch leagues in the 20th century) made it sixteen teams in 1998. But it all started with these original eight:

CHICAGO WHITE STOCKINGS	NOW THE CHICAGO CUBS, NOT THE WHITE SOX. I KNOW, IT'S CONFUSING.
NEW YORK MUTUALS	POOR GAME ATTENDANCE LED TO FINANCIAL PROBLEMS. THEY COULDN'T FINISH THE 1876 SEASON AND WERE KICKED OUT OF THE LEAGUE. DISBANDED IN 1876.
BOSTON RED STOCKINGS	CURRENTLY THE ATLANTA BRAVES. YEAH— ANOTHER CRAZY ONE. NOT THE PRESENT-DAY BOSTON RED SOX. GO FIGURE.
HARTFORD DARK BLUES	MOVED TO BROOKLYN. DISBANDED IN 1877; FINANCIAL ISSUES.
PHILADELPHIA ATHLETICS	SAME FATE AS THE NEW YORK MUTUALS.
ST. LOUIS BROWN STOCKINGS	LASTED ONLY TWO SEASONS. FOLDED IN 1877 WHEN THEY SIGNED LOUISVILLE GRAYS PLAYERS JIM DEVLIN AND GEORGE HALL. UNFORTUNATELY, DEVLIN AND HALL WERE INVOLVED IN A GAMBLING SCANDAL THAT TOOK DOWN THE WHOLE TEAM.
CINCINNATI RED STOCKINGS	PRESENT-DAY CINCINNATI REDS. APPARENTLY STOCKINGS WERE A THING BACK THEN.
LOUISVILLE GRAYS	OPERATED FOR ONE SEASON.

Like Father, Like Son

THE ONLY FATHER-AND-SON DUO IN THE HALL OF FAME

Can you imagine having a mom or pop who's an All-Pro, All-Universe, superstar athlete who has set all sorts of records, then *you* come along and do just as well? The National Baseball Hall of Fame in Cooperstown, New York, has more than 300 inductees. Of all the names of pioneers and record breakers, there are two names unlike any others. They are **LARRY MACPHAIL SR.** and **LEE MACPHAIL**, the first father-and-son duo to be inducted into the Hall of Fame.

Larry MacPhail Sr. grew up in a small town in Michigan, the son of a banker with rather large pockets. The elder MacPhail founded and owned over twenty banks. So, yeah—fat pockets. Larry didn't become a banker. He graduated from George Washington University Law School and took a gig with a law firm in Chicago. Later he became a department store executive in Nashville, and even served in World War I.

After the war, Larry started his own law firm and became an owner of the Columbus Red Birds, a minor league squad for the St. Louis Cardinals. While with the Red Birds, he came up with really creative ways to draw a crowd, like installing floodlights for evening games, building a new stadium, and introducing special ticket packages for women and children. He did such a great job that in 1934, the Cincinnati Reds hired him as their general manager.

The Larry MacPhail Award, established in 1966, is given to the minor league squad with the best promotional efforts. In 2018, the Eugene (Oregon) Emeralds won the coveted award. They had thirty-two promotional theme nights, like STEAM Night for kids interested in computer or engineering careers and '80s Throwback Jersey Night for the nostalgic old-school fans.

In that position, Larry showed the same pioneering spirit he had in the minors. His team was the first to fly to road games, and he developed some of the earliest protective batting helmets and helped create healthcare benefits for players and retired players. And on May 24, 1935, he introduced the first night game in Major League Baseball.

Larry MacPhail's son Lee MacPhail was also an influential MLB executive. After graduating from Swarthmore College, Lee worked his way up in minor league baseball, and served as the director of player personnel for the New York Yankees from 1948 to 1958. His job was to create a productive and successful farm system to train young high school and college players to play for the Yankees. Lee's efforts contributed to nine pennants and seven world championships for the Yanks.

In 1959, Lee became the general manager of the Baltimore Orioles. Before Lee, the closest thing they had to a winning season was in 1957 when they finished with a 76–76 record. But in his seven years with the team, Lee helped the Orioles achieve a .547 winning percentage.

Larry MacPhail was inducted into the Baseball Hall of Fame in 1978. In 1998, Lee joined him. Like father, like son.

I GET IT FROM MY POPS!

Although the MacPhails are the only father-and-son pair in the Baseball Hall of Fame, there are other duos who have made major contributions to the sport. Here are a few that you may want to know about. Really . . . these guys are awesome:

★ Possibly the best father-and-son pitching pair, **MEL AND TODD STOTTLEMYRE** had a combined 302 wins and racked up 2,844 strikeouts. Mel Stottlemyre was a five-time All-Star over his eleven-season career with the New York Yankees between 1964 and 1974. He also won five World Series rings, not as a player, but as a very effective pitching coach (one with the New York Mets and the other four with the New York Yankees). His son, Todd Stottlemyre, was a top pick in the 1985 MLB draft, and he won two world championships with the Toronto Blue Jays in 1992 and 1993.

★ The first father-and-son duo to ever play on the same game-day roster was **KEN GRIFFEY SR.** (at the age of forty) and **KEN GRIFFEY JR.** (at the age of twenty) on August 31, 1990, against the Kansas City Royals. The elder Griffey had a pretty good nineteen-year career, mostly with the Cincinnati Reds. He was one of the leaders of the Big Red Machine: the Reds team that dominated the National League from 1970 to 1979. Griffey Sr. won two World Series titles with the Reds in 1975 and 1976. He was also a three-time All-Star. He finished his illustrious career in 1991 with the Seattle Mariners, where he played second fiddle to baseball's new superstar, his own son, Junior.

Ken Griffey Jr. has gone down in league history as one of the best center fielders of all time. "The Kid" had all the tools: fielding, throwing, plus a high batting average and POWER. I'm talking thirteen-time All-Star, ten-time Gold Glove winner, American League MVP, and seven-time Silver Slugger winner (given annually in both leagues to the best offensive player in each position). Junior played for twenty-two seasons and was elected to the Baseball Hall of Fame on January 6, 2016. Both father and son are in the Cincinnati Reds Hall of Fame.

★ Though he won the first two of his seven MVP awards in his early years with the Pittsburgh Pirates, **BARRY BONDS** is mostly known for his record-setting years with the San Francisco Giants. His father **BOBBY BONDS** played there first, though (obviously). Between them, they have seventeen All-Star appearances, eleven Gold Gloves, and they're both on the San Francisco Giants Wall of Fame.

THE LOWEST ERA
IN MLB HISTORY

Here's a little math for ya:

The formula to calculate a pitcher's Earned Run Average (ERA) is earned runs (any runs that occur without some kind of error in the field, like a botched catch) multiplied by total innings in a game (which is usually nine, duh) divided by the number of innings that the particular pitcher actually pitched. In other words:

$$\frac{\text{EARNED RUNS} \times \text{TOTAL INNINGS}}{\text{NUMBER OF INNINGS PITCHED}}$$

Now, why is this important? This formula is used to determine how good a pitcher is. The lower the ERA, the better the pitcher. No one wants to be the guy who gives up a gaggle of runs on his watch. You want to be the guy who doesn't give up any hits and allows zero runs. In fact, you want to be a guy like Hall of Famer **ED WALSH**, who has the lowest career ERA of all time, 1.82.

Big Ed played in the majors for fourteen years—thirteen years

for the Chicago White Sox and one lone season for the Boston Braves (the present-day Atlanta Braves) from 1904 to 1917. (His first two years with the Sox, his ERA was 2.37.) Then his White Sox teammate Elmer Stricklett taught him a sloppy, icky secret: the spitball (see page 48). In 1906, Big Ed threw spitballs regularly and became the top dog of the pitching staff. He ended the season with a winning record of 17–13 and had an ERA of 1.88. He went on to help the Sox win the World Series that year as well—striking out seventeen batters in fifteen innings. Walsh's ERA stayed under 2.00 for the next four years thanks, in part, to the spitball. In 1908, he won a record forty games, a number of victories that hasn't been reached since—and probably never will be again.

Despite all of Big Ed's wins, many baseball experts place an asterisk by his name. Some say that because he pitched in an era when the spitball was legal, his low ERA shouldn't count. Today, not only are spitballs illegal, but balls are switched out regularly so they're always clean. The league also dropped the pitcher's mound 5 inches after the 1968 season, making the strike zone smaller. With all these changes, it's kind of hard to compare a pitcher from the late 1880s to a superstar of today. And if women, Black, and Latinx players had been allowed to play major league ball back then, increasing the level of competition, how would Ed have fared? We'll never know.

THE
HIGHEST-SCORING
GAME EVER!

Can you imagine a baseball game with a total of 49 runs? Doesn't sound real, does it? Well, my friend, it happened. Yes, it did. On Friday night, the 25th of August in 1922, before a crowd of 7,000 at the old Chicago Cubs stadium, the appropriately named Cubs Park.

The Cubs hosted the Philadelphia Phillies, and it was electric. For starters, neither squad was particularly good. (The Cubs were competitive, but they finished fifth in their division that year with an 80–74 record. The Phillies were abysmal—they finished the season that year with a 57–96 record. Yikes!) In fact, the bats were lively because the pitching was so bad. The two Phillies pitchers gave up 25 hits and 26 runs, including 3 home runs. The Cubs trotted out five pitchers, led by Tony Kaufmann. He gave up 9 hits and 6 runs, but at least no one on the Cubs pitching staff gave up a homer.

RADICAL RECORDS

The top hitters in the game were Cubs left fielder Hack Miller, center fielder Cliff Heathcote, and shortstop Charlie Hollocher. The trio combined had 12 hits, 10 runs, and 16 RBIs. Hack even had 2 of the 3 home runs. Their bats were popping, but not consistently. The Cubs only scored 1 run in the first, 10 in the second, 14 in the fourth, and 1 more in the sixth.

The Phillies almost came back by scoring a whopping 14 runs in the eighth and the top of the ninth, but they couldn't pull it out. Chicago won 26–23.

The very next day, both teams faced each other again. They were exhausted, and it showed. The score remained 0–0 for ten straight innings. The Phillies, ready for this to end, scored 3 runs at the top of the eleventh, making the final score 3–0. Fifty-seven years later, on May 17, 1979, these two franchises met again and attempted to top the record set in 1922. It was another crazy, high-scoring, horrible day for pitchers. The Phillies won this time, 23–22, four runs shy of tying the record.

SALARIES
AND THE FIRST MILLION-DOLLAR MAN

On March 2, 2019, it was announced that MVP right fielder and ex-Washington National Bryce Harper signed with the Philadelphia Phillies for the largest contract in North American sports history—**330 MILLION** bucks over thirteen years! You read right. $330 million. But check this out—a month later, Los Angeles Angels center fielder Mike Trout signed a contract that eclipsed Harper's little deal. It was for a ridiculous **$426.5 MILLION** over twelve years! Can you believe that? That's what you call BIG money. But there wasn't always so much money in baseball. Let's rewind.

In the 1920s, baseball was not a big business, and salaries were much lower than they are now—some players were paid less than $3,000 a year. Most major leaguers had side gigs to supplement their incomes. Some sold insurance, some worked at hardware stores, others were car mechanics.

But as baseball's popularity grew, there were opportunities for teams (and the players) to bring in more money. Teams raised ticket prices, sold toys and t-shirts, and were sponsored by corporations in exchange for advertising at games. But the thing that really pumped up that baseball cash was the rise of television in the 1950s and 1960s.

In 1946, the Yankees became the first team to sell local television broadcast rights to their games, bringing in an extra $75,000 for the team. More teams followed, and soon anyone could experience a ball game from the comfort of their own home.

Over time, as the money rolled in, players wanted to make sure they got a fair share. In 1966, the Major League Baseball Players Association (a union for major leaguers) was founded to protect the rights of athletes. Two years later, a historic collective bargaining agreement (the first of its kind in all of sports history!) was signed between Major League Baseball and the MLBPA. It ensured that contracts for all major league players were standardized and guaranteed players a minimum annual salary of $10,000.

When Red Sox pitcher Babe Ruth (that's right, he wasn't always a Yankee or a power hitter) was traded to the New York Yankees in 1919, he doubled his annual salary for the next two years, from $10,000 to $20,000. Then in 1922, he signed a contract for the next two seasons that paid him an average of $50,000 a year. That was almost unheard of back then! From 1922 until he retired in 1935, Babe remained the highest-paid player in the game.

Now fast-forward to today: The television broadcast rights for Yankees games sell for $100 million. In 2018, Major League Baseball made a record revenue of $10.3 billion. How did baseball go from $10,000 player salaries to Mike Trout's staggering $426.5 million contract, all in only about fifty years? Advertising.

With television, advertisers—you know, the people who make commercials for burgers and pimple cream—could reach more people than they ever had before. They were willing to pay big bucks for a chance to tell you about their products during a major league game.

The better the players, the better the team. The better the team, the more fans tune in, and the more potential customers there are for advertisers. So players' salaries get higher and higher as teams try to keep or recruit top talent, in order to bring in more fans and the big advertising bucks.

Most salaries aren't as high as Mike Trout's or Bryce Harper's, but in this big money game the best players are in high demand. Millions of dollars may seem like a lot for a bunch of guys just playing baseball, but the players are what baseball is all about—they are the ones doing the work, drawing the crowds, and bringing money to the sport.

If you work hard, you deserve a fair cut of the money and every single dime that comes your way.

THE
MOST- AND LEAST- ATTENDED GAMES
IN MLB HISTORY

odger Stadium in Los Angeles and RingCentral Coliseum in Oakland can safely accommodate over 50,000 loyal, screaming, hot-dog-and-peanut-scarfing fans. Tropicana Field in St. Petersburg, Florida, has the lowest capacity in the major leagues, with just over 31,000 seats. But the most-attended game ever happened in a place that wasn't even built for baseball. And the least-attended game happened while a city was in pain.

In 2008, the Los Angeles Dodgers celebrated the fiftieth anniversary of their move to LA from Brooklyn. To celebrate, they played an exhibition game against the Boston Red Sox in the famed Los Angeles Memorial Coliseum. Originally built for track and field and football games, the Coliseum was home to the Dodgers from 1958 to 1961. On March 29, 2008, a record **115,300 FANS** came to watch the Sox win, 7–4.

At the other end of the spectrum, the least-attended game in MLB history happened on April 29, 2015. That day, the Baltimore Orioles played the Chicago White Sox in Oriole Park at Camden Yards. With no one watching.

Earlier that month, on April 19, a twenty-five-year-old Black man named Freddie Gray died from severe neck and head injuries he suffered while in police custody. Thousands of Baltimore citizens reacted, and the city erupted in violent protests. The Sox and the Orioles played as scheduled, but the game was closed to the public for safety concerns. The Orioles won, 8–2.

Before the Baltimore game, the lowest number of people to attend a game was six. Six people came out on September 28, 1882, for a game between the Troy Trojans of New York and the Worcester Ruby Legs of Massachusetts. The mighty Trojans won that day, 4–1. Why didn't more people show up? Well, to put it plainly, both teams stunk. They were so bad, they weren't allowed back in the league the following season. Yikes.

THE
ONLY MAN NAMED MVP
IN BOTH LEAGUES

MVP. Most valuable player.

That's the one. The one and only. The player who puts up the sickest numbers and the most unbelievable stats. The one the fans want to see. Each year since 1931, the Baseball Writers' Association of America has voted on the one player in each league who stands out from the rest. Only one man was super-powered enough to win the award in both the American and National Leagues: **FRANK ROBINSON**.

Mr. Robinson was a star from the start. As a rookie with the Cincinnati Reds in 1956, he hit 38 home runs, tying the rookie home-run record. That year, he was seventh on the list to win the MVP award, an All-Star, and the National League Rookie of the Year.

By 1961, Robinson was feared by pitchers and infielders alike. He loved to crowd that plate, daring pitchers to hit him. And he tore up the baselines, barreling toward the men guarding the bases, wanting them to think twice about trying to tag him out.

That season, Robinson led the Reds to the National League pennant and ended the season with 37 homers, 124 RBIs, 176 hits, 117 runs scored, 22 stolen bases, and a .323 batting average. Naturally, he was named the National League's Most Valuable Player.

In 1965, the Reds traded Robinson away to the Baltimore Orioles, an American League team. The Reds thought he was an old-timer at the age of thirty, and that his best days were behind him. But they gave up on the brother too soon. The next season was arguably the best of Mr. Robinson's career.

In 1966, Robinson hit 49 home runs, had 182 hits, 122 runs scored, 122 RBIs, and held down a .316 batting average. He won the Triple Crown, which is given to the player who leads the league in three very important offensive categories: RBIs, homers, and batting average. He did it all. Mr. Robinson won the American League MVP trophy with first place votes from every writer who voted. Bet the Reds wished they had held on to "grandpa" Frank!

Over the course of his career, Robinson hit 586 home runs and was a fourteen-time All-Star. His #20 jersey was retired with three clubs: the Indians, Orioles, and Reds. And he was a pioneer off the field as well. In 1975, he became the manager of the Cleveland Indians, making him the first Black manager in major league history. He later managed the San Francisco Giants, Baltimore Orioles, Montreal Expos, and Washington Nationals. He was inducted into the Baseball Hall of Fame in 1982.

The first MVP award was given in 1910 by the Chalmers Motor Company. They offered one of their most luxurious cars, the Chalmers Model 30, to the major league player with the highest batting average. They ended up giving out two cars that year—one to Ty Cobb of the Detroit Tigers, the other to Napoleon Lajoie of the Cleveland Naps (today's Cleveland Indians)—because of some funny math and maybe some not-so-ethical ball playing.

THE FASTEST RECORDED
PITCH
SO FAR . . .

In the comic book world, superheroes run as fast as the speed of sound. I bet they could outrun the fastest pitch that ever left the hand of a mortal. Maybe they could even *throw* pitches with amazing speed. That'd be cool to see, right? Well as far as we know, the two major league pitchers with the fastest pitches ever are not superheroes come to life. They just throw that heat harder than anyone has before.

If you've ever seen Cuban-born New York Yankee pitcher Aroldis Chapman, you understand why fans call him "the Cuban Missile" (awesome superhero name). During the 2010 season, while Chapman was with the Cincinnati Reds, his pitch was clocked at **105.1 MPH**! It's officially a Guinness World Record.

In 2016, Chapman matched his own record. The next year, he threw 44 of the top 50 fastest pitches, and the top 23 were all his! How sick is that? But in 2018, a rookie from the St. Louis Cardinals showed that he might have what it takes to become the fastest arm in the biz.

Jordan Hicks made his major league debut on March 29, 2018. He displayed his Herculean right arm right away, and became known for his "sinker" (a fastball with kind of a downward spin; it causes the batter to hit grounders), "slider" (something between a fastball and a curved pitch that breaks down and away from a right-handed hitter), and a pitch called a "four-seam fastball," which is the fastest, straightest pitch that a pitcher can muster. Hicks's four-seamer gets up to 102 mph on average. But on May 20, 2018, against the Philadelphia Phillies, he tied Chapman's 105.1 mph record. Throughout that season, Hicks owned the fifty fastest pitches list. Chapman was only listed nine times, and his fastest pitch was 104.4 mph. Our boy Jordan? He was on the list thirty-nine times! The top two places are his: two 105 mph pitches on the same day. Jordan Hicks and Aroldis Chapman are the only, THE ONLY, pitchers in MLB to reach 105 mph.

PLAYERS WHO HIT A

Grand Slam

THEIR FIRST TIME AT BAT

What would it be like to come up from the minors to play in a major league ballpark, something you've been dreaming of all of your life, and in your first at bat . . . you send the ball soaring over the center-field wall? Or even better, you did it on the very first pitch?! Think it can't get any bigger than that? Think again. What if you send the ball flying out of the park when all three bases are loaded? That's called a grand slam—it's a very rare thing, and even rarer for a debut batter to accomplish. In fact, in the entire history of Major League Baseball, only four players have ever hit a grand slam their first time up to the plate.

BILL DUGGLEBY was most notably a pitcher for the Philadelphia Phillies. They called him "Frosty Bill." Some say it was because he seemed to pitch better in chilly conditions. Others say it was because he just wasn't much of a talker. If that's true, I'm sure he had much more to talk about when, during his very first time at bat, he smashed a home run into orbit with all three bases loaded. It happened on April 21, 1898, off New York Giants pitcher Cy Seymour, and it was the first time a guy hit a grand slam his very first time at bat. The Phillies went on to defeat the Giants 13–4.

Duggleby only hit 5 more home runs in his eight-year career. He might not have been a home run king, but he did hold down that grand slam record for a mighty long time. The next guy to hit a grand slam his first time at bat was **JEREMY HERMIDA**, 107 years later.

Hermida, a right fielder for the Florida Marlins, hit his debut grand slam on August 31, 2005, against the St. Louis Cardinals. Of the four players who hit a grand slam on their first try, he is the only one to accomplish the feat as a pinch hitter—in other words, a substitute. The bases were loaded in the bottom of the seventh and the Cardinals were up 10–0. The Marlins were able to muster up one more run in the bottom of the eighth, but still lost 10–5.

RADICAL RECORDS

The next time a guy hit a grand slam his first time at bat was on September 2, 2006. Cleveland Indians third baseman **KEVIN KOUZMANOFF** started his rookie campaign in amazing fashion by hitting a grand slam on his first-ever pitch in the first inning. "I got a good pitch, up in the zone . . . hit it out of the park," said Kev. His entire family was there to watch him add his name to the MLB record books. Just a day earlier, he had been an up-and-coming star in Triple-A baseball on a team in Buffalo, New York.

On June 12, 2010, the Boston Red Sox called a kid named **DANIEL NAVA** up from the Triple-A Pawtucket Red Sox to replace outfielder Josh Reddick. Nava swung at the very first pitch thrown his way. With the bases loaded, he popped the ball with all he had, and it flew over the wall in right field. It was the bottom of the second inning, and the Sox took the lead over the Phillies. They kept their lead for the rest of the game and won 10–2.

There have been plenty of first at bat homers since Daniel Nava joined the grand slam foursome. But no other first-timer to date has hit a homer with the bases fully loaded. Who knows? You could be next. Get to work on that power swing!

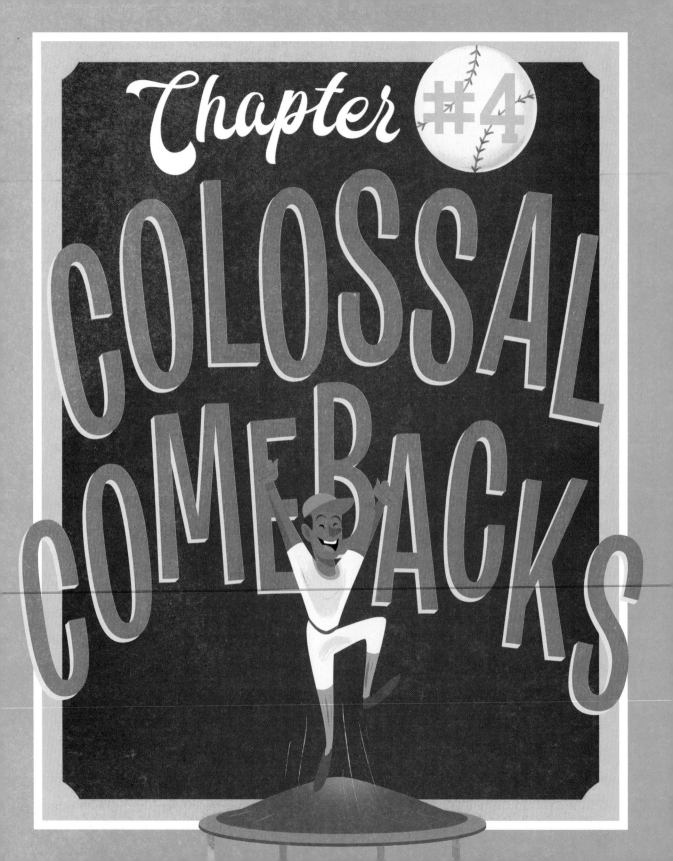

**B**aseball is a game of strategy and patience. Of course, you've got to have the tools—a few heavy hitters, a couple hot pitchers, and a team of gritty ballplayers ready to put in the work—but you need more than all that when you're competing against the best of the major leagues. You need fire. Enough fire to keep fighting even when the odds are against you. Even when the other team has so many runs, a win seems impossible. Even when doctors tell you your playing days are over. Baseball is all about that fire—getting on your feet, screaming yourself hoarse, *just in case*, just in case it makes a difference. Because sometimes, it does.

Sometimes the comeback happens right away; sometimes it takes over one hundred years. Those squads who bounce back unexpectedly are called "Cinderella" teams. But there are no glass slippers here, only champions.

The 1906 **CHICAGO CUBS** were Goliaths. With outstanding pitching from Mordecai Brown (check out his story on page 26)—who had a ridiculous 1.04 ERA that year, and only gave up 1 homer in thirty-six games—it's easy to see why they were the National League champions. Left-handed pitcher Jack Pfiester also played a huge role in the Cubs' dominance, leading the team with 153 strikeouts. Plus, their hitting was thunderous. They led the league that year with 1,316 hits, thanks to batters like outfielder Frank Schulte, third baseman Harry Steinfeldt, and first baseman Frank Chance. The Cubs' regular season record—116 wins to 36 losses—gave them a winning percentage of .763, the highest percentage of wins ever.

The American League champions that year were the **CHICAGO WHITE SOX**. The White Sox were not the powerhouse team their crosstown rivals were—they came in dead last in the American League with a .230 team batting average. In fact, a reporter for the *Chicago Tribune* dubbed them the "Hitless Wonders." At the end of July, the Sox were in fourth place in the AL, behind the Philadelphia Athletics, the New York Highlanders, and the Cleveland Indians. But those teams started losing, and the Sox had a winning streak in

August that changed their season. From August 2 to August 23 they played nineteen straight games without a loss and eight of those nineteen wins were shutouts.

The pitching during that run was superb. The Sox's star pitcher was "Big Ed" Walsh. He was a spitballer with a 1.88 ERA for the season. Fellow future Hall of Famer Sam Crawford once said of Walsh's pitches, "I think that ball disintegrated on the way to the plate and the catcher put it back together again. I swear, when it went past the plate it was just the spit that went by." The Sox also had two guys who had won twenty games apiece that season—Frank Owens and Nick Altrock—and the league's ERA champ, Doc White, with a cool 1.52. But would pitching be enough for them to slay the giants that were the Cubs?

The first game of the best-of-seven series was played at the West Side Grounds, the home of the Cubs. Surprisingly, the White Sox pulled out a 2–1 victory behind the masterful pitching of Nick Altrock. The Cubs won the second game, 7–1, at South Side Park III, the home of the Sox. The next two games were shutouts: The Sox won the third game 3–0, and the Cubs won the fourth game 1–0. The series was now tied two apiece. Would it be pitching or hitting that brought the championship home? Spoiler alert, it came down to some heavy hitting, just as many thought it would. Just not from the team they expected.

In Game 5, the White Sox, the supposed Hitless Wonders, opened up a can of lively bats and won 8–6. In Game 6, the Cubs tried to rally, but the Sox won again, 8–3, and took home the title! Why did the Sox suddenly start hitting with fire? Some of it had to do with the fact that Cubs ace pitcher Mordecai Brown was exhausted from pitching two complete games. But some of it was just plain old desire, will, and "want to" on the part of the White Sox. All season, everyone who followed the Sox had known them as a squad that couldn't swing the lumber. Well—surprise! They were still pro baseball players with a lot of pride, and it showed that day.

The Sox and their fans on the South Side of Chicago will always have this victory to hang over the heads of Cubs fans. The Sox defied expectations, showing the world you can't ever put anyone, or any team, in a box.

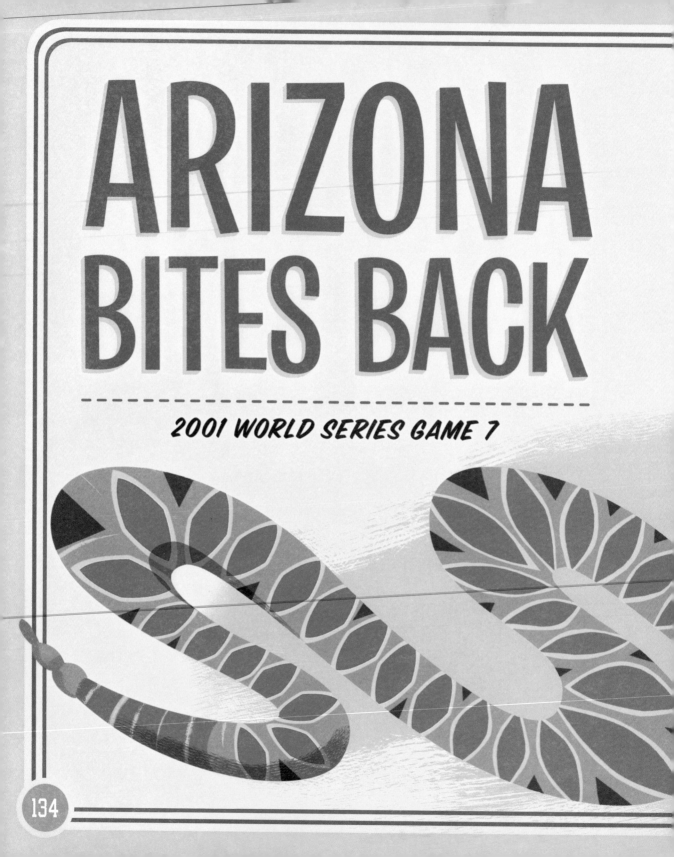

ARIZONA BITES BACK

2001 WORLD SERIES GAME 7

Game 7 in a World Series is every baseball fan's dream game. Both teams are tied three games apiece and are only one game away from making history. This is it—each team's last shot to prove they're champions. Usually there's one team that's heavily favored to win. But don't tell that to their opponents—especially if they have venomous fangs.

The 2001 World Series was between two well-matched teams: the Arizona Diamondbacks (92 wins, 70 losses) and the New York Yankees (95–65). The Yanks had won the last three World Series championships, making them the favorite.

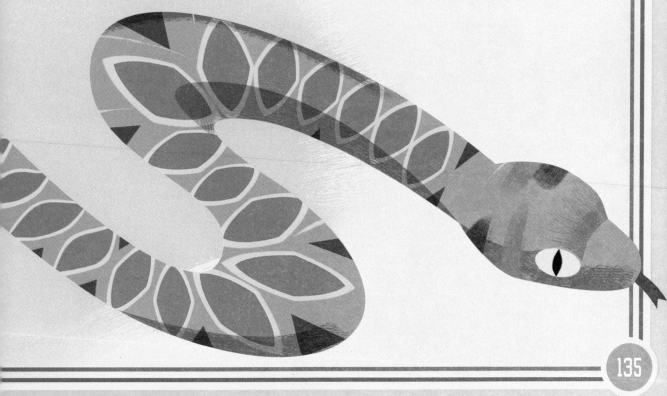

But the Diamondbacks, named after one of the deadliest snakes in America, entered the series like they were the big rattlers on the diamond.

Usually the World Series starts in mid-October, but because of the terrorist attacks on September 11, the championship was delayed by a week. The first game was played on October 27, 2001, and the Diamondbacks won. They won the second game the next day.

New York City was the site of the largest terrorist attack, so when Games 3, 4, and 5 came to New York just seven weeks later, it boosted the morale of the entire country. The Yankees won all three games—the highest attended in the series—thanks in part to some All-Star-caliber pitching from "the Rocket," Roger Clemens, and Sterling Hitchcock.

Game 6 was back in Phoenix, and everyone had counted the D-backs out. Everyone but the Diamondbacks themselves. Diamondback pitcher (and future Hall of Famer) Randy Johnson started, and he did not disappoint. "The Big Unit," as Johnson was called, pitched seven innings and only gave up 2 runs. The bottom of the third inning is when the game turned around for the D-backs. Led by center fielder Danny Bautista and right fielder

Reggie Sanders, Arizona banged out 8 runs. The Yanks never recovered. The final score of Game 6 was 15–2 and the series was tied.

The D-backs and the Yanks trotted out even more ace pitchers in Game 7. The D-backs' Curt Schilling pitched brilliantly for eight straight innings, but gave up a home run to Alfonso Soriano in the top of the eighth. The Yanks were now up 2–1. It looked as if they were about to win another championship. They brought in the best relief pitcher in the game, Mariano Rivera, to pitch the last two innings.

Rivera started off by striking out two of Arizona's toughest batters. But it all went awry in the bottom of the ninth when he gave up a single, then made an error fielding a bunt attempt, putting runners on first and second base. The next batter up, Tony Womack, hit a double and drove in a run, tying the game 2–2. Rivera hit the next batter with a pitch, and just like that, the bases were loaded. Next up was Luis Gonzalez, who hit a beautiful walk-off floater to center field, driving the runner on third home. The score was 3–2. The game was over. The Diamondbacks were World Series Champs.

KEEP ON TICKING

JOHN HILLER'S RETURN

JOHN HILLER was an amateur pitcher in Canada when the Detroit Tigers' scouting department discovered and signed him in 1962. He didn't get much playing time until 1967 when the Tigers decided to use him in every imaginable pitching capacity—as spot starter, closer, middle reliever, you name it. He was a pivotal part of Detroit's 1968 world championship team as well, with a 2.39 ERA and a 9–6 record. John was becoming one of Detroit's best pitchers. But after the 1970 season, while in northern Minnesota, he had a frightening experience that not only threatened the rest of his career but could have ended his life.

On the morning of January 11, 1971, while having breakfast, John felt a sudden pain in his neck and chest, and what felt like a bolt of lightning shot up his arms. Within an hour, John had suffered a massive heart attack and two smaller attacks. This was a serious health scare, but John refused to let the 1970 season be his last. After surgery and a stringent rehabilitation and

weight-loss regimen he returned to the Tigers in 1972. At first, the Tigers offered him a coaching position and a chance to pitch to the batters during practice. But John begged, pleaded, and demanded to be put on the mound again. On July 8, 1972, against the Chicago White Sox, John got his wish. He gave up 4 hits, 2 runs, and had a sad 6.00 ERA. But he was just getting warmed up. He fared much better in his next forty-one innings, only allowing 8 earned runs. He ended the year with 3 saves, 26 strikeouts, and a phenomenal 2.03 ERA.

John came roaring back the following season and had his best ever. He pitched in sixty-five games in the 1973 season, the most of any pitcher in the league that year. He had a 10–5 record, posted the lowest ERA of his career (an awesome 1.44), and gave the Tigers a record-setting 38 saves. On top of all of that, he finished fourth in the Cy Young (an annual award given to the best pitchers in the NL and AL) and MVP voting. Many sportswriters and baseball historians consider John's 1973 season one of the best seasons ever by a relief pitcher.

Altogether, John played nearly eight seasons after his health scare. He ended his career with 125 saves and 1,036 strikeouts. What a comeback!

TEN BIG RUNS

THE LARGEST SINGLE-GAME POSTSEASON COMEBACK IN MLB HISTORY

n 1929, the **CHICAGO CUBS** and the **PHILADELPHIA ATHLETICS** were shoo-ins for the World Series. Both teams were number one in their respective leagues for almost the entire season. The Cubs ruled the National League and finished the season with a 98–54 record. The Athletics finished the season with an even better record: 104–46. Fans thought the World Series would be a slugfest, but what really happened was a lot more interesting.

Game 1 was at Wrigley Field, the home of the Cubs. The Cubs' batters were no match for the A's ace pitcher Howard Ehmke. He pitched the entire first game, and his changeup (or slow) pitches and wicked sidearm delivery were perfect. The A's won 3–1.

In Game 2, the A's worked the Cubs over with their hitters. In all, the A's tallied 12 hits and 9 RBIs and won again, 9–3. Game 3 was played in Philly at Shibe Park. It was a much smaller venue than Wrigley, but A's fans came out in large numbers to cheer their team on. The game was a defensive struggle. Cubs pitcher Guy Bush, "the Mississippi Mudcat," pitched a beautiful game and only gave up 1 run, shutting down the Athletics after the sixth inning. His efforts sealed the deal and got the Cubs their first win of the series; the final score was 3–1.

The next night, Saturday, October 12, 1929, still beaming from Game 3, the Cubs got off to an 8–0 lead in Game 4. They scored 2 runs in the fourth, hammered out 5 in the sixth, and added 1 more for good measure at the top of the seventh. The Cubs just needed 9 more outs to win the game and tie up the series. It was the bottom of the seventh and what came next not only made history, it was given a name—the "Mack Attack," after the Athletics manager, Connie Mack, one of the winningest managers in baseball history.

Athletics left fielder Al Simmons sparked the attack with a homer. The score was now 8–1. From there the A's went on a hit fest. They scored 3 more runs, cutting the Cubs' huge lead in half. With two A's on base, center fielder Mule Haas hit an inside-the-park homer, making the score 8–7. After a walk and a single, first baseman Jimmie Foxx drove in a run that tied the score, 8–8. One hit batsman later, the bases were loaded again. Philadelphia infielder Jimmy Dykes drove in 2 runs, and the A's took the lead, 10–8. They never let it go.

Philadelphia's 10-run comeback is the largest to date in postseason history. The A's went on to win Game 5 with a score of 3–2, and with that, the World Series. It was their first title in sixteen years.

The Return of
TONY C.

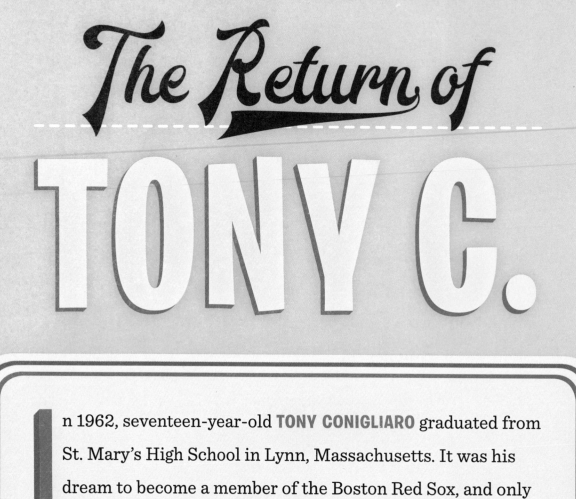

n 1962, seventeen-year-old **TONY CONIGLIARO** graduated from St. Mary's High School in Lynn, Massachusetts. It was his dream to become a member of the Boston Red Sox, and only months after graduation, he signed a contract with his favorite squad. For one season, Tony trained in the Class A New York–Penn Minor League. In the 1963 season, he hit 24 homers and had a .363 batting average. He played so well that he made his rookie debut with the Boston Red Sox the next year, at the age of nineteen.

In 1964, his first season, Tony had 117 hits, 52 RBIs, a batting average of .290, and 24 home runs. His hitting stance and the way

he attacked the ball were perfect, but because he crowded home plate, he was hit by a ton of pitches. On July 26, in a game against the Cleveland Indians, one of those pitches broke his arm, and he didn't return until September 4.

In 1965, Tony led the league with 32 home runs. Two years later, he played in his first All-Star game. He was on his way to becoming a Red Sox great, but on August 18, 1967, in Fenway Park, his career and life changed forever.

In the bottom of the fourth inning, Tony stepped to home plate for his second chance at bat. Angels pitcher Jack Hamilton heaved a killer fastball that seemed to get away from him. Tony C. tried to duck like he had done so many times before, but the ball hooked and headed straight for his head at full speed. The ball smashed into the left side of his face, narrowly missing his temple. It shattered his cheekbone, permanently damaged his eye, and dislocated his jaw.

Many thought that the twenty-two-year-old's career was over. When the swelling went down and discoloration went away, Tony was left with blurred vision in his left eye. But the next season, he proved he could still smash it over the wall. He had 20 homers,

82 RBIs, and 129 hits. And he won the Sporting News Comeback Player of the Year Award in 1969. In 1970, he drove in more runs (116) than in any other season of his career. Tony's comeback was short-lived, though. His vision continued to get worse, and he was just never the same player he once was. In 1975, he left the game for good.

In 1983, helmets with ear flaps became part of the major league uniform. In 2013, after years of trying to perfect the headgear, the league required batters to wear a special helmet made from aerospace-grade carbon fiber that is supposed to protect them from pitches up to 100 mph.

In the brief time that Tony C. did play, he made a huge, positive impact on Red Sox Nation. The Red Sox even instituted an annual award named in Tony's honor. The Tony Conigliaro Award is given to "the Major Leaguer who has overcome adversity through the attributes of spirit, determination, and courage that were trademarks of Tony C."

ROOKER

PROMISE

n June 8, 1989, the sixth-place Philadelphia Phillies hosted the fifth-place Pittsburgh Pirates in a regular season match of two cellar dwellers (i.e., teams at the bottom of their divisions). They played a night game at Veterans Stadium in front of only 18,511 fans. Yeah. It was that bad. To make matters worse, the lowly Phillies were riding an eleven-game losing streak coming into this match-up. They started off this game miserably as well, digging themselves into a deep hole that looked impossible to climb out of.

This is how quickly it got out of hand: First, the Phillies walked

151

Pirates outfielder Barry Bonds. Then, after a quick ground ball out, three batters hit singles. Boom. 2–0, Pirates. Then Pirates first baseman Jeff King walked and shortstop Rey Quiñones hit a double. Boom! 4–0, Pirates. After another walk, the pitcher Bob Walk drove in 2 more runs, and the score was 6–0. Barry Bonds came back and smacked a homer, bringing in 3 more runs. Boom! 9–0. The next batter grounded out. Now there were FINALLY 2 outs! The pain was almost over. The next batter hit a single. The batter after him walked. Outfielder Gary Redus hit a single and drove in another run. BOOM! The Pirates were up 10 to nothing . . . in the top of the first inning!

Things looked so good for the Pirates that **JIM ROOKER**, a former pitcher for the Pirates and their current radio announcer, infamously said, "If the Pirates lose this one, I'll walk home to Pittsburgh." In the bottom of the first inning, Phillies first baseman and right fielder Von Hayes hit a 2-run homer. Uh-oh. 10–2, Phillies. Then Hayes came back around in the third inning and hit another 2-run dinger over the wall. Uh-oh. 10–4. Second baseman Steve Jeltz got in on the 2-run homer-fest and belted one out in the fourth inning. Uh-oh. 10–6.

In the top of the fifth, the Pirates picked up another run on an Andy Van Slyke double, making it 11–6. After a couple of walks, Jeltz hit his second home run, driving in 3, then pinch hitter Ricky Jordan brought in another run. 11–10, Phillies. Then John Kruk singled in the eighth inning, followed by 2 walks, and scored on a wild pitch, tying the score. 11–11!

At this point, that harmless little bet that Rooker made didn't seem so harmless anymore.

After a 2-run single by Darren Daulton, the Phillies finally took the lead, 13–11. Right fielder Curt Ford knocked a weak pitch deep to left field for a triple and brought in the two guys on base. Altogether, the Phillies scored 5 runs at the bottom of the eighth inning. And that was it. The final score? 15–11, Phillies.

Jim Rooker was speechless, but he kept his word. He and a good friend, Carl Dozzi, began the 310-mile hike on October 5, 1989. They walked in the rain, over a mountain range, and averaged 24–30 miles a day. It took thirteen days, but "Jim Rooker's Unintentional Walk" raised over $85,000 for the Bob Prince Charities and the Pittsburgh Children's Hospital.

ERIC THE RED FIGHTS BACK

Los Angeles native **ERIC DAVIS** is what you might call an outfielding phenom. During his seventeen-year career (1984–1994; 1996–2001), he spent nine seasons with the Cincinnati Reds, thus the nickname "Eric the Red." (Also a reference to the Norse explorer Erik Thorvaldsson, famous for settling Greenland and being the dad of another Norse explorer, Leif Eriksson, but I digress.) Eric was impressive. He became a Gold Glove winner, an All-Star, and a World Series champion. But he was also plagued by many health problems, from sore joints to injured kidneys. He always

bounced back. Even when he faced one of the greatest health scares of all.

Davis's career started when he was drafted by the Reds in 1980. He debuted in his first major league game in 1984, and from there racked up impressive stats and athletic feats. For example: In the first half of the 1987 season, he hit 27 home runs, had 68 RBIs, and was batting .321. Three years later, he helped the Reds upset the Oakland Athletics in the World Series. But because of his health and injuries he bounced from team to team. He landed with the Dodgers for parts of 1992 and 1993 and the Tigers in 1993 and 1994.

In '96, the Reds gave him another chance. He felt better than he had in a long time, and his numbers showed it. He had 26 home runs, 83 RBIs, 119 hits (batting .287), and had stolen 23 bases on top of that. He did so well that at season's end, he won the Sporting News Comeback Player of the Year Award and earned a big contract with the Baltimore Orioles, playing for them in the 1997 season.

But in May of '97, Davis experienced some of the worst stomach pain he'd ever had. It was so bad he couldn't even stand up. He went to the hospital, where he was diagnosed with colon cancer. He immediately had surgery to remove the mass, and after a month of rest, began working out again.

Part of his recovery included chemotherapy treatments that made him very tired. But he battled through the fatigue and continued to work out like a mad man. On September 15, 1997, while still undergoing chemotherapy treatments, Davis made his biggest comeback yet. He took the field. He only played in one game of a double-header against the Cleveland Indians and didn't make much of an impact, but he was back on the field. He played in forty-two games that year and was determined to return the next season.

The season of 1998 was one of Davis's best ever. He had 148 hits, knocked the ball out of the park 28 times, had 89 RBIs, and the fourth best batting average in the AL with .327. He was even named the Players Choice Comeback Player of the Year.

Davis retired for good in 2001. He ended his career with 934 RBIs, 282 home runs, and 349 stolen bases. He was inducted into the Cincinnati Reds Hall of Fame in 2005.

WILLIE'S
ICONIC CATCH

THE BEST CATCH BY THE BEST FIVE-TOOL PLAYER OF ALL TIME

Hall of Fame center fielder **WILLIE MAYS** of the San Francisco and New York Giants is considered by many sports and baseball historians to be the best five-tool player of all time. A five-tool player is a very rare athlete who excels in base running, fielding, throwing, hitting for average, and power hitting. Willie could do it all. Running the bases? Mr. Mays stole 338 in his career. Throwing and fielding at his position? He won twelve Gold Glove awards at center field and had 195 outfield assists. That means that 195 times in his career he successfully launched the ball back infield and threw an opposing player out.

Hitting for average? He retired with an awesome .302 batting average with 3,283 career hits. Hitting for power? He had 660 home runs in his career. Willie was bad (meaning "good")!

But there was one play that many say proved he was the best all-around baseball player of all time: the Catch.

In 1954, the Cleveland Indians faced the New York Giants in the World Series. The first game in the series was very defensive. Both squads refused to give up the big hits or easy runs. But in the top of the eighth inning, the score tied 2–2, Cleveland's Vic Wertz was up to bat. He was a formidable hitter; not a huge threat, just someone Cleveland could rely on. Wertz got ahold of a pitch by the Giants' Don Liddle and sent that ball screaming some 420 feet to center field. Then All-Star center fielder Willie Mays did the unthinkable.

The ball was heading deep into center field, which at the Polo Grounds was a farther distance than in most ball parks. With his back to the ball, Mays raced to get ahead of it, then arched his back and caught it over his left shoulder. Then he spun around and quickly threw the ball into the infield. The fans couldn't believe what they had just seen. They were on their feet, cheering for the "Say hey" kid.

That catch was amazing in part because of the shape of the Polo Grounds. At 483 feet from home plate, the center field wall was insanely far away. (By comparison, the distance from center field to home plate in current-day Yankee Stadium is 408 feet.) The center field was so deep that runners often scored from second base because it took so long for a throw to reach home plate. But on that day, Mays adjusted perfectly and made a play that most players at his position had never successfully performed. Why? Because they weren't Willie Mays, that's why.

Mays himself was less impressed by his catch and more impressed by his throw to the infield. There was a runner on first and a runner on second, and neither of them made it home.

If not for Mays's amazing play, the Indians might have won the series. The G-Men from New York went on to win the game 5–2 and swept the championship, winning four straight games.

OVERCOMING
THE CURSE *of the*
BAMBINO

The Boston Red Sox won five World Series championships between 1903 and 1918, but 1918 would be the last time they'd wear the crown for another eight decades. The dry spell from 1918 to 2004 is known by many Red Sox faithful as the **CURSE OF THE BAMBINO**. But where did the spell come from? Here's the tale:

Babe Ruth was called "the Bambino" (meaning "baby" in Italian). It was a nickname for a nickname as his real name was George. He started his major league career with the Boston Red Sox. He was such a superb pitcher that he helped them win

three championships. Babe was also a powerful hitter, with 49 home runs and 224 RBIs between 1914 and 1919. Boston fans loved him, so no one could have imagined that Red Sox owner Harry Frazee would sell Ruth to the Yankees (they were not the bitter rivals they are today, but many think this trade was the start of the over one-hundred-yearlong feud). But that's just what Frazee did on December 26, 1919.

After the trade, the Yankees won championship after championship, bagging twenty-seven in all—four while Babe was part of the team. But no matter how they tried, the Red Sox couldn't make it to the promised land. Oh, they were close a few times, in '46, '67, and '75, and super close in '86. But close doesn't get you a World Series ring.

The 2004 Red Sox finished the season with a 98–64 record, right behind the Yankees in their division. They had All-Star players like David Ortiz, Johnny Damon, and Manny Ramírez, and superstar pitchers like Curt Schilling and Pedro Martinez.

Fittingly, they played the Yankees in the playoffs, and lost the first three games. For Game 3, in Fenway Park, the home of the Red Sox, the Yanks blasted the boys from Boston with a final score of 19–8. Every baseball fan on the planet knew that Game 4 would probably be more of the same and that New York would win its twenty-seventh World Series title. But the Red Sox climbed out of that hole and ended up winning the next four games and the AL championship. They were the first and, to this day, the only Major League Baseball team to come back from a three-game deficit in a seven-game series. And how cool was it that they beat the team that took Babe Ruth? They were World Series–bound!

The Sox ended up sweeping the St. Louis Cardinals in four games. DING DONG, THE CURSE WAS FINALLY DEAD! The Sox won the World Series again in 2007, 2013, and 2018, stomping the curse into oblivion. It took them eighty-six years to break the curse, but the comeback of the mighty Boston Red Sox as a championship organization was huge. Babe Ruth–sized huge.

For years, Red Sox fans would travel to the gravesite of Babe Ruth and bring him offerings of flowers and alcohol, attempting to lift the wicked curse. But the only thing that worked was patience and some really good baseball.

That's the
BALLGAME!

So, by now your brain should be all pumped up with newfound, invaluable knowledge to share. Big ol' muscle brain, jam-packed with baseball info that only a top graduate with a PhD from Baseball University would know. Yeah, if that were a real college, you'd be on the dean's list, buddy. I'm telling you.

When Kim Ng becomes the first woman in major league history to be hired as a general manager and lead a dynasty, you can say you knew her when. You know all about dudes like Royals great George Brett, "Wonder Kid" Joe Nuxhall, and "Humongous Shoe-in-Mouth Guy" Jim Rooker.

Hopefully, you have some idea of how much of a challenge it was for players of color, players from outside the United States, and for women to be part of this beautiful game. To just play and prove to the world how awesome they are.

Baseball has evolved since its humble beginnings. Hopefully it will continue to evolve in big ways. No more spitballs, right? That's big. Men of all backgrounds playing together. That's even bigger. But when will women be allowed on the field? Sometime soon, I hope.

And you know what? Maybe one day we'll play ball on the moon. In a luxurious stadium, complete with sky box suites so high up you'll have a clear and gorgeous view of Earth as the ball soars over the wall and floats out into the galaxy. It could happen.

In the meantime, now that you have all these names and stats and records floating around in your noggin, you know who got game?

You, that's who.

ADDITIONAL TIPS & RESOURCES

Adamson, Thomas K. *Baseball: The Math of the Game*. Capstone. 2011.

Davis, Mo'ne. *Remember My Name: My Story from First Pitch to Game Changer*. HarperCollins. 2016.

Finch, Jennie. *Throw Like a Girl: How to Dream Big & Believe in Yourself*. Triumph Books. 2011.

Gramling, Gary. *The Baseball Fanbook: Everything You Need to Know to Become a Hardball Know-It-All*. Sports Illustrated Kids. 2018.

Jacobs, Greg. *The Everything Kids' Baseball Book: From baseball's history to today's favorite players—with lots of home run fun in between*. Everything. 2018.

Mochizuki, Ken. *Baseball Saved Us*. Lee and Low. 1993.

Nelson, Kadir. *We Are the Ship: The Story of Negro League Baseball*. Jump At The Sun. 2008.

Tocher, Timothy. *Odd Ball: Hilarious, Unusual, & Bizarre Baseball Moments*. Two Lions. 2014.

COVER YOUR BASES WITH THESE SITES:

Baseball Hall of Fame
baseballhall.org

Society of American Baseball Research
sabr.org

Baseball Reference
baseball-reference.com

The Official Site of Major League Baseball
mlb.com

GLOSSARY

ALL-STAR/ALL-STAR GAME: An All-Star is the player in each position that fans and other players decide is the best. National League and American League All-Stars play against each other in the All-Star Game in the middle of the season.

BATTING AVERAGE: A way of measuring hitting performance, it's the number of hits divided by a player's total at-bats. A fantastic batting average is .300—or three hits for every ten at-bats. Hitting in the major leagues is *that* hard!

BOX SCORE: A chart that summarizes each team's stats, including home runs, walks, strike outs, and runs scored.

BUNT: A hit that occurs when a batter turns his or her bat horizontally and taps the ball into the infield, often with the idea of advancing runners on base.

CHANGEUP: An off-speed or slow pitch meant to trick the batter into swinging too early.

CURVEBALL: A breaking pitch (or a pitch that does not travel in a straight line) that moves downward toward the plate.

CUTOFF: When an outfielder throws the ball to an infielder (aka the cut-off man), who then throws the ball to the appropriate base for the out.

CY YOUNG AWARD: An honor given to the best pitcher in the American and National Leagues. It is voted on by members of the Baseball Writers' Association of America.

EARNED RUN: A run that counts against a pitcher because of the offensive team at bat and not because of an error in the field.

ERA: Stands for "Earned Run Average" and is an important way of measuring a pitcher's performance. It's the average of earned runs allowed per nine innings pitched. Good pitchers have low ERAs.

FASTBALL: The straightest, fastest pitch in the game. This is the most basic pitch but can be the hardest to throw well because of its speed!

FIVE-TOOL PLAYER: A very rare athlete who excels in base running, fielding, throwing, batting average, and power hitting.

GENERAL MANAGER: The businessperson responsible for building and running a team. The GM is basically the boss of the organization, making all the tough decisions, from trading players to signing free agents.

GRAND SLAM: A home run when there are runners on all three bases (aka, the bases are loaded). The hitter gets four RBIs (or Runs Batted In) for this type of home run.

GROUND INTO A DOUBLE PLAY: When a batter hits a ground ball that results in an out for the batter and a baserunner.

HIT FOR THE CYCLE: When a batter hits a single, a double, a triple, and a home run in one game, in no particular order.

KNUCKLEBALL: A rare pitch with little-to-no spin that moves so slowly it seems to dance across home plate.

MAJOR LEAGUE BASEBALL PLAYERS' ASSOCIATION: An organization that negotiates for better player salaries and working conditions.

MVP: Stands for "Most Valuable Player." It is an award given to a player (in each league) for their outstanding performance throughout the season.

"NATURAL" CYCLE: When a player has four hits in order: a single, double, triple, and then a homer.

NEGRO NATIONAL LEAGUE: An all African American league started in 1920. It was the first of its kind to last for more than one year.

NO-HITTER: When a pitcher does not allow one hit in a single game. (However, batters can still get on base because of a walk, an error, or if they are hit by a pitch.)

ON-BASE PERCENTAGE: A number that measures how often a batter gets on base.

OUTFIELD ASSIST: When an outfielder throws the ball to an infielder and makes an out.

PERFECT GAME: When a pitcher retires every batter in order, without one batter reaching base in any form.

PINCH HITTER: A person who comes off the bench to replace another hitter in the batting order.

PINE TAR: A sticky material that makes the bat easier to grip. But too much of it is illegal.

RBI: Stands for "Run Batted In" or "Runs Batted In." A batter "bats in" a run when his or her at-bat results in a runner crossing home plate.

SACRIFICE FLY: When a batter hits a fly ball to the outfield, deep enough for a runner on third base to score or to advance a runner at another base. This player sacrificed his or her at-bat for the good of the team, and the out does not count against his or her batting average.

SAVE: A relief pitcher (or a non-starting pitcher) comes out of the bullpen to "close out" the game in the ninth inning or later. The relief pitcher earns a "save" if he or she keeps the lead and their team wins the game.

SCREWBALL: One of the toughest breaking pitches (a pitch that does not travel in a straight line) to throw. It moves to the right for a right-handed pitcher and to the left for a left-handed pitcher. If the pitcher and batter are both righties, the ball breaks toward the batter. If the pitcher is a righty and the batter is a lefty, the ball breaks away from the batter.

SINKER: A fastball with a downward spin. It usually causes the batter to hit grounders.

SLIDER: A pitch between a fastball and a curveball that breaks down and away from a right-handed hitter, when thrown by a right-handed pitcher.

SLUGGING PERCENTAGE: The total bases divided by the number of times the player was at bat.

SPITBALL: A ball that a pitcher coats with spit to make it move in unpredictable ways. It's now illegal.

STOLEN BASE: When a baserunner moves up a base without being advanced by a hit or walk.

STRIKEOUT: When a batter receives three strikes, either by swinging and missing, hitting a foul ball, or taking a called strike by the umpire. The symbol for a strikeout is "K" or a backwards "K" if the hitter is "caught looking" (instead of swinging) at strike three.

STRIKE ZONE: The area over home plate between a batter's shoulders and their knees. If a pitch falls within this area, it is called a strike by the umpire at home plate. But each umpire has a different view of the strike zone!

SWITCH HITTER: A player who can bat from both sides of the plate (either righty or lefty!).

TRIPLE CROWN: A title given to the player who leads the league in three very important offensive categories: RBIs, home runs, and batting average.

UTILITY PLAYER: A player who can play multiple positions in the field.

WALK: When a pitcher throws four balls, or four pitches outside of the strike zone, and the batter doesn't swing at any of them. After the fourth pitch, the batter "walks" to first base.

WALK-OFF: When the home team, in the bottom of the ninth inning or later, scores enough runs to either break a tie or come from behind to win. When the winning run is scored, the game is over and both teams can "walk-off" the field.

ABOUT THE AUTHOR

DERRICK BARNES is the winner of the 2018 Ezra Jack Keats Book Award for outstanding new writer, and his picture book *Crown: An Ode to the Fresh Cut* took home four honors at the 2018 American Library Association's Youth Media Awards: the Coretta Scott King Author Honor and Illustrator Honor, the Newbery Honor, and the Caldecott Honor. Derrick is also the author of the *New York Times* bestselling picture book *The King of Kindergarten*, and the bestselling chapter book series Ruby and the Booker Boys. Derrick lives in Charlotte, North Carolina, with his wife, Dr. Tinka Barnes, and their four sons, all of whom play sports.

ABOUT THE ILLUSTRATOR

JOHN JOHN BAJET is a Los Angeles—based visual development artist working in animation and picture books. He has worked as a color stylist in animation for *The Tom and Jerry Show*, as well as online PBS Shorts. Past clients include Hasbro, Scholastic, PI Kids, and Cottage Door Press. To see more of his work, visit *johnbajet.com*.